OKLAHOMA CITY UNIVERSITY SCHOOL OF LAW

COME TO LEARN.
LEARN TO LEAD.

OKLAHOMA CITY UNIVERSITY SCHOOL OF LAW

COME TO LEARN.
LEARN TO LEAD.

BY LEE PEOPLES AND BOB BURKE

FOREWORD BY THE HONORABLE RONALD J. NORICK

Series Editor: Gini Moore Campbell
Associate Editor: Natalie Taylor

OKLAHOMA HALL *of* FAME

PUBLISHING

Printed in Canada.
ISBN: 978-1-938923-46-3
LCCN: 2020906838
Designed by Skip McKinstry
UNLESS OTHERWISE NOTED, PHOTOGRAPHS ARE COURTESY OF THE OKLAHOMA CITY UNIVERSITY SCHOOL OF LAW

CONTENTS

FOREWORD
A GLORIOUS PAST—A BRILLIANT FUTURE

Come to Learn. Learn to Lead., written by Lee Peoples and Bob Burke, is a wonderful history about one of the most historic buildings in Oklahoma City, designed by one of Oklahoma's most celebrated architects, Solomon Andrew Layton. Not only did Layton design this building, he also designed more than a dozen buildings in Oklahoma City, including the Skirvin Hotel and Tower, the Oklahoma County Courthouse, and the Oklahoma State Capitol. This is a story about a building that was opened in 1910 as Oklahoma City's first high school after the citizens of Oklahoma City approved a bond issue to fund the construction. The high school's name was changed to Central High School in 1920 and operated as Central High School until 1968 when the last graduating class of 133 received their high school diplomas.

This magnificent building has not only educated many students, but has also served as the headquarters for several prominent corporations including Southwestern Bell Telephone and Oklahoma Farmers Union Mutual Insurance Company. The readers will be reminded this historical building was also the command center for the Alfred P. Murrah Federal Building Bombing that took the lives of 168 Oklahoma citizens on April 19, 1995.

As this story is told, the reader will recognize many graduates' names who contributed to the extraordinary growth of Oklahoma and Oklahoma City. You will read about the politicians and business leaders who insisted Oklahoma City's children have the best education possible and were willing to support this goal. I'm sure, if those citizens were here today, they would be pleased to learn this once proud high school will be a place of learning for decades to come.

I'm proud Solomon Andrew Layton's magnificent structure is once again a school of learning for future generations.

Ronald J. Norick

Oklahoma City University Board of Trustees Chairman (2010-2019)
Mayor of Oklahoma City 1987-1998

PREFACE
THE CAPITAL CITY IS OUR CAMPUS

In 2008, Bob Burke and Von Creel published *Oklahoma City University School of Law: A History.* Dean Lawrence Hellman wrote the closing chapter predicting that the next stage of the school's history would "involve the creation of new, more expansive facilities, perhaps in downtown Oklahoma City." Dean Hellman envisioned a "signature building … part of an architecturally-advanced complex that would strengthen the ties between the law school and the profession and society it serves." Partnerships between the school and law-related organizations would flourish and experiential learning opportunities could be expanded in a downtown location.

The predictions made by Dean Emeritus Hellman have become reality as the school has settled into its magnificent downtown campus over the past four years. The school launched a new series of programs in 2017 called Capital City Connect to strengthen relationships between current students, alumni, and friends in the legal community. The inaugural year featured six unique programs focused on the school's most active centers and certificate programs: health law, state and local government, energy law, estate planning, homeland security, and public interest law. Each program was co-chaired by a faculty member and a distinguished practitioner with expertise in the relevant subject matter area. The programs connected second and third year law students with members of the practicing bar before graduation. Each program examined current substantive issues in the practice area and also provided networking and career development opportunities.

The school's prominent location and variety of meeting spaces have attracted a number of events that have enriched the student experience. The annual Alfred P. Murrah Summit on Homeland Security Law brings leaders from across the nation to the school to discuss recent developments in the field. A workshop entitled Protecting Houses of Worship brought hundreds of leaders from the local faith community to the law school to explore how religious freedom can be strengthened by protecting houses of worship. "Civility Matters" was presented to attorneys and students by Chief Judge of the Oklahoma Supreme Court Douglas Combs (OCU Law '76) and other distinguished alums to address the decline of civility in the legal profession. Each year the school's Distinguished Practitioners in Residence and Jurists in Residence deliver public lectures and host roundtable discussions that contribute to the academic community. The school will continue to offer captivating discussions and events that enrich student learning and development.

Jim Roth '09 was the speaker for the 2017 OCU Law alumni lunch at the Oklahoma Bar Association annual meeting. Roth became the 13th Dean of the School of Law on July 1, 2018.

A grant from the Oklahoma Bar Foundation enabled the school to launch the Housing Eviction Legal Assistance Program in 2018 to reduce the eviction rate in Oklahoma City. Under the guidance of an attorney director, students are trained to assist Oklahomans facing eviction from their homes. Students learn and apply the relevant laws, gain client communication and counseling skills, draft legal pleadings, and appear in court. The program was launched with the encouragement of the Oklahoma County judiciary who oversee the extremely busy eviction docket. The program is modeled on the school's pro-se waiver divorce docket program which continues to thrive. A grant from the Inasmuch Foundation in 2019 helped sustain the work of the Housing Eviction Legal Assistance Program.

The school's legal externship programs have benefited from our longstanding relationships with courts, governmental agencies, corporations, non-profits, and other legal employers. Externship placement sites will continue to expand due in part to the school's convenient location in the heart of the downtown legal community.

The law school was a visionary among the state's institutions of higher learning in moving downtown and we are grateful for the work of Dean Emeritus Valerie Couch who helped make it happen. Following our arrival in 2015, the University of Oklahoma's College of Business relocated to the nearby Health Sciences Center and the University of Central Oklahoma opened a downtown location three blocks south of the law school.

The law school's downtown location has been and will continue to be useful in strengthening the relationships that other OCU colleges and departments have with businesses, governmental agencies, and the non-profit community in downtown Oklahoma City. OCU pre-law courses are scheduled in classrooms at the law school to give OCU undergraduates a taste of what life is like in our downtown building. The law school hosts events for other OCU colleges and departments to enhance their connections with the surrounding community.

In the spring of 2019, the OCU Law Alumni Association was relaunched to help keep our graduates connected to one another and the school. Another exciting recent development is the launch of the Bail & Bond Clinic. This innovative clinic will connect students and the Public Defender's Office with qualifying Clients who have

The school's eviction assistance program was featured on the front page of *The Oklahoman*.

otherwise suffered long pre-trial Jail stays simply because of unnecessary high bails and bonds. The Bail & Bond Clinic was initiated under a grant from The E.L. and Thelma Gaylord Foundation supporting a new Criminal Justice Center at the Law School.

The school is exploring new opportunities to provide legal education through legal masters degree programs. These new offerings appeal to a growing segment of the workforce desiring some training in law without obtaining a Juris Doctor degree. The classroom capture technology installed in every classroom will be harnessed to deliver portions of these programs online to students in remote locations.

Our move downtown represents a return to our roots as a downtown law school operating in several downtown locations from the 1930's – 1950's. Returning to the city's core has allowed us to further strengthen our historical connections to the practicing bench and bar. Our flexible scheduling options attract a diverse student body whose wide range of life and work experiences enrich the educational environment. The school's multitude of externship opportunities, clinics, and partnerships with courts and humanitarian organizations allow students to develop critical legal knowledge and skills while serving society. Often our students can even walk to court or their jobs with ease because we are at the heart of the city. Dean Hellman's prediction that a move downtown "would reflect the law school's engagement with social issues affecting the entire community" has become reality. Oklahoma City University School of Law serves justice by molding servant leaders.

I thank Bob Burke and Professor Lee Peoples for their stewardship to this building. In this book, they have beautifully captured its history and its people. They show us that a mighty spirit lives here. And in this place, we proudly move forward in the spirit of progress — where tradition, innovation, leadership and service define both our heritage and our future.

Jim Roth

Dean and Professor of Law, Oklahoma City University School of Law
OCU LAW CLASS OF 1994

FROM THE PRESIDENT

OCU Law provides a world-class education in the classroom, but the training for a career in law does not stop there. Opportunities abound to work with real clients on pro bono cases in clinics and to gain practical knowledge through internships with law firms and government agencies. We are so fortunate that the location of OCU Law places it in the center of Oklahoma City's legal scene. OCU Law is a great place to launch a legal career.

Martha Burger

President, Oklahoma City University

DEDICATION

The authors dedicate
OKLAHOMA CITY UNIVERSITY SCHOOL OF LAW
COME TO LEARN. LEARN TO LEAD.

to Dean Emeritus and Professor of Law Valerie Couch.

During her five years of service as Dean, she worked tirelessly to advance

the School of Law. The school's awe inspiring new home is the

physical representation of her abilities and success as Dean.

Shortly after her installation as the school's twelfth Dean,

Valerie learned that the University was considering acquiring the building.

She thoroughly immersed herself in the large and small details

of the building's acquisition, design, renovation, fundraising,

and the actual physical move. The law school quite simply

would not be in its beautiful new home without her immense efforts.

On behalf of past, current, and future faculty,

staff, students, and alumni —

Thank You Valerie!

OKLAHOMA CITY UNIVERSITY SCHOOL OF LAW

COME TO LEARN.
LEARN TO LEAD.

1 AN HISTORIC CONNECTION BEGINS

The histories of Oklahoma City University and the iconic downtown landmark, Central High School, were inexorably intertwined from the beginning. The band from Epworth University, the University's original name, provided the music for the ceremonial laying of the 10,000-pound granite Masonic cornerstone of the new high school building on November 28, 1909. In addition, Epworth Chancellor George H. Bradford was the first on a short list of dignitaries to address the crowd gathered for the historic ceremony. As Central High School became the cornerstone in public education in Oklahoma, Oklahoma City University's influence on higher education began to take shape a few miles to the northwest at Northwest 23rd Street and Blackwelder Avenue.

For the first 21 years of Oklahoma City's existence, high school students did not have a permanent school with sufficient space to accommodate the influx of new families. Oklahoma Station, later named Oklahoma City, was "born grown," reaching a population of nearly 6,000 before nightfall on April 22, 1889, the day the Land Run opened for settlement of two million acres in central Oklahoma that had not been assigned to American Indian tribes occupying much of the future state.

Until a public school system could be formed and funds acquired to build public school buildings, students attended subscription schools in which parents paid one dollar monthly per student directly to the teacher. The teacher, normally a woman because of the low pay, was required to find a place to hold classes. Lyman and Martha North opened a school with 70 students in a tent after the Land Run. Jennie Sutton also opened a school in the rear of a hardware store on First Street between Broadway and Robinson avenues.

Subscription schools began to diminish after the Organic Act of 1890 established Oklahoma Territory and allowed citizens to form local school districts. In 1892, the Oklahoma City School Board established a school that offered high school classes in a rented, one-room storefront on California Street. The Myriad Botanical Gardens sits on the spot of the city's first public school. Mary Couch, 22 years old and married but a year, was the teacher. Only a few advanced courses were taught for high school-level learners. Most students across the country attended school through the eighth grade, and high school was reserved for those learning skilled trades or preparing for college.

Because of segregation, separate schools were provided for black

Artist Xiang Zhang's depiction of the Oklahoma Land Run of 1889, a painting in the private collection of Tom and Judy Love. *Courtesy Xiang Zhang.*

students. Traditionally underfunded, the first black high school classes were held in a small building in the present location of the Chickasaw Bricktown Ballpark.

Recognizing the need for a full high school curriculum, socialite Julia Douglas, who also founded the city's first public library, organized a citizens' committee to promote high school teaching excellence. In 1893, the high school for white students was moved to an abandoned building on Military Hill, the Federal Military Reservation at Northeast Fourth Street and Walnut Avenue. At the time of the Land Run of 1889, the U.S. War Department built several barracks, stables, and other structures to house the contingent of soldiers that enforced the law until Oklahoma City could form a central government and hire a police force. By 1893, the federal presence was no longer necessary as city and territorial laws

The first business established at Oklahoma Station, later called Oklahoma City, was a flour and feed store owned by farmer C.A. McNabb. *Courtesy Oklahoma Historical Society.*

authorized police agencies, and ownership of the Military Hill land was again under control of local authorities.

The school on Military Hill was austere and roughly-built. Historian Ethel McMillan wrote:

> The four-room log houses had been used as a barracks on the Military Reservation. It was here that young people were given the opportunity to learn and become productive citizens of the society.

There was no public school transportation system. Usually, students arrived on foot, bicycle, or, occasionally, a pony. When fire destroyed the school building on the Military Reservation in 1894,

the third year of public high school classes was held in a Methodist church at 119 Northwest Third Street. The church later became St. Luke's United Methodist Church. In 1895, the building at Northwest Fourth Street and Walnut Avenue, commonly known as the Irving Building, was occupied as "Oklahoma City High School."

Even though the new building, built near the site of the burned-out school on the Military Reservation, was used as Oklahoma City's high school for ten years, it never was officially named for Washington Irving, the famous author of such tales as *Sleepy Hollow* and *Ichabod Crane* who visited the future state of Oklahoma in 1832 and wrote a detailed description of its land and inhabitants.

Even before statehood, there was talk about building a large, permanent high school just north of downtown. There was good reason. The Irving Building had long been insufficient for the growing number of students. In March, 1907, the high school had 600 students. Many of them were housed in classrooms built in vacant buildings adjoining the school grounds. It was also necessary to hold two separate schools, a morning session and an afternoon session.

The School Board had purchased eight lots at the corner of Northwest Seventh Street and Robinson Avenue. The city was expanding northward, but much of the land north of Eighth Street was made up of corn fields and pastures. A majority of the members of the School Board believed that the location was ideal for a centrally-located high school. To provide funds to build the school, it was necessary for voters to approve a building bond issue. At a community meeting at the India Temple in early October, 1907, members of the Chamber of Commerce and School Board voiced opinions that at least $500,000 should be allocated to building a new high school and other junior high and grade schools. A resolution was passed to move forward with the bond issue "to induce people to relocate here on account of the exceptional educational advantages."

However, inaction followed even though the number of high school students was growing by nearly 20 percent per year. Oklahoma became the 46th state of the Union on November 16, 1907, and Oklahoma City's high school continued to "burst at the seams."

With more than 800 high school students enrolled in early 1908, citizens clamored for the long-proposed new high school. Citizen groups and business leaders appeared at regular meetings of the School Board to demand action. Finally, the School Board called for

The first graduating class of Oklahoma City High School. *Courtesy Harn Homestead & 89er Museum.*

The Irving Building served as the high school for a decade and later as the temporary State Capitol. *Courtesy Oklahoma Historical Society.*

a bond issue election on November 3, 1908. The bond issue, which contained money for both public schools and hospitals, provided $300,000 for construction of the high school. To promote the passage of the bond issue, the Chamber of Commerce paid for 4,000 buttons that proclaimed, "Vote for the Bond Issue and the new High School."

Classes were dismissed on Election Day to allow young men of the high school to "button hole" voters and ask them to vote "yes." Because laws of the new state did not allow general election officers to preside over school question balloting, tents were set up adjacent to regular polling places in which patrons were asked simply to vote "yes" or "no." Upon exiting the tent, all men who voted for the school bonds were given a tag that read, "I voted for the school bonds, did you?"

The Daily Oklahoman strongly editorialized in favor of the bond issue:

> We can ill afford to have it known abroad
> that we are not properly housing our scholastic
> population. We cannot hope to attract home
> seekers and investors with such an impression. We
> had better, therefore, stand for an inconsequential

Architect Solomon Layton made an early impact upon public buildings in Oklahoma. *Courtesy Oklahoma Historical Society.*

increase in taxes in order to build an adequate high school building and at the same time serve notice upon the world that we are first in public school facilities.

Voters overwhelmingly approved the bond issue, and the School Board immediately began to search for an architect to develop plans for a modern high school. Members of the Board expressed the desire to include in the high school a club room, swimming pool, gymnasium, and an auditorium to seat 1,500.

The School Board chose the architectural firm of Layton, Wemyss-Smith, and Hawk. The firm's principal architect was Solomon Andrew Layton. Born in Iowa into a family of carpenters and builders, Layton founded his architectural firm in Oklahoma City in 1902 and practiced for 41 years until his death in 1943. He and his partners shaped the early character of Oklahoma, designing more than a dozen multi-story buildings in downtown Oklahoma City, including the Skirvin Hotel and the Skirvin Tower; 16 county courthouses, including the Oklahoma County Courthouse; and eventually buildings at Oklahoma City

THE HIGH SCHOOL'S REAL NAME???

Many have been confused about the correct original name of the High School. Newspapers and alumni often referred to the school as "Oklahoma High School." However, until other high schools were built, the official name of the school was "Oklahoma City High School." That name appeared on diplomas, in yearbooks, and on the masthead of the first edition of the school newspaper, *Sooner Spirit*, in 1921.

University; the University of Oklahoma campus in Norman; and the Oklahoma Medical Center in Oklahoma City. Partially based upon his elegant design of Oklahoma City High School, often referred to as Oklahoma High School, Layton later was chosen to design the Oklahoma State Capitol.

In May 1909, the School Board approved Layton's plans for the new high school. The plans called for the stone structure to be 210 feet by 154 feet and to contain four floors. With the design approved, the Board began accepting bids for construction. The Masonic cornerstone was laid on November 28, 1909.

After years of political infighting over the hiring of the city's school superintendent, the School Board showed unanimity in selecting Dr. W.H. Brandenburg of Mason City, Iowa, as superintendent in January 1910, at a salary of $3,000 per year. Brandenburg earned degrees from Columbia University in New York and was a highly respected educator.

From the beginning, he recognized that Oklahoma City High School could not be built for the $300,000 in bonds originally approved by voters. On April 5, 1910, school patrons voted 2,929 to 504 to provide another $150,000 in bonds to complete the building and to buy equipment and furniture.

Oklahoma City was gaining population, including school children, at such a fast pace, some leaders called it the "fastest growing city in the Southwest." In 1910, city fathers approved a comprehensive plan to improve the quality of life for its residents. Included was the construction of a boulevard to encircle the city. Much of that circle, Grand Boulevard, still can be traveled around the city today.

Even though construction of the new high school was months from completion, two events were held in the building in May 1910. The Class of 1910, whose members had campaigned for approval of the bond issue, was allowed to hold graduation ceremonies in the unfinished structure. In addition, public school teachers from around the county met from late May to the middle of June in the building for instruction in what was called the Oklahoma County Normal Institute.

"High School is Near Completion" was the headline in *The Daily Oklahoman* on November 18, 1910. The first classes were held in the building two months before at the beginning of the school term. The 50 instructors worked around plumbers, painters, and decorators who were daily working long shifts to complete the structure. The newspaper story was optimistic:

Nearly 1,100 students are anxiously awaiting the days when the artisans shall have placed the finishing touches on the interior of the new high school and banish from the corridors the noise of the hammer and the buzz of the saw.

By Christmas 1910, the high school still was not completed. A newspaper story reported that the gymnasium was far from ready and that the exterior of the building would be sand-blasted by a newly-invented machine which would put a finished look to the stone. Because the building still was under construction, the School Board put off any formal dedication.

2 THE NEW HIGH SCHOOL

It is the finest building in the state. GOVERNOR LEE CRUCE

Finally, the last painting and lacquering of the gymnasium floor was completed and the School Board opened the new Oklahoma High School to the public. On March 3, 1911, the building was formally dedicated as 5,000 people toured the structure and 1,600 gathered in the auditorium for a long session of speeches. When Governor Lee Cruce, Superintendent W.H. Brandenburg, and School Board member W.A. Clement entered the auditorium, the 25 men sitting on the stage and the large audience broke into applause. Cruce had toured the building and had nothing but good things to report. He said:

> This is the finest school building in Oklahoma, the finest building in the state. But it takes more than names and brick and mortar to make a school. It takes the proper faculty and the proper pupil.

Other dedication speakers included Superintendent Brandenburg who quoted a passage from the Bible, "God shall make the desert to bloom like a rose," to describe the new high school building. He said, "If God ever made the desert bloom, he has done so in Oklahoma, but only because of the sacrifice of many servants who made this building possible." Brandenburg said he had visited the finest high schools in Boston, Chicago, Milwaukee, and St. Louis, and that Oklahoma High School was "as good or better" than anything he had seen in the nation.

High School Principal Professor F.C. Jacoby told the audience that in seven years the high school student body had grown from 301 to 1,350, the faculty had increased from 10 to 48, and the city's population had topped the 100,000 mark for the first time. Future federal judge Edgar S. Vaught, a graduate of the high school, said he had closely inspected the building and was satisfied that the School Board had wisely invested $500,000 in taxpayer funds to construct such a fine structure.

The new high school was architecturally impressive, a mixture of classical and gothic styles. The exterior walls were limestone blocks with classical and gothic features. There were large common areas, classrooms, and

Judge Edgar S. Vaught.

high ceilings. Substantial glass allowed natural light to flow into the halls and classrooms. The large auditorium, well-equipped trade and science laboratories, and a modern gymnasium were highlights of the completed construction.

In addition to a new building, the administration and faculty provided an innovative night school for 450 students who held full-time jobs during the daytime and completed their high school work at night. Night school students ranged in age from 14 to 35. The progressive program caught the attention of educators nationwide. A newspaper account noted that among the night students were a stone cutter, a brick mason, several telephone operators, grocery wagon drivers, and janitors.

In May 1911, the Oklahoma High School graduating class was the largest in the city's history. Of the 105 graduates, 67 were female and 38 were male. At that time in education history, it was not unusual for a majority of high school graduates to be young women. Young men often quit school early and went to work.

Before the fall term in 1911, Superintendent Brandenburg and Principal Jacoby announced a radical change in the course of study at the high school. The idea was to make the curriculum "more practical, to prepare the student for his or her life's work, rather than for college." Because only 25 percent of graduates continued their education at a college or university, the Oklahoma City education plan was in line with other school districts in the nation.

Oklahoma High School athletic teams, the Cardinals, scored well against area competition. Dressed in red and black uniforms, 40 track and field prospects competed for spots in dual meets

The new Oklahoma City High School Building in 1913. *Courtesy Oklahoma Historical Society.*

The hallway outside the school auditorium was elegantly decorated and contained photographs of historic events of the school and its students. *Courtesy Oklahoma Historical Society.*

with other central Oklahoma high schools. Under the watchful eye of high school athletic director and football coach, Dr. H.H. Cloudman, the football team beat El Reno 22-0 in the first game of the 1911 season. The win was made possible by trick plays and use of the relatively new forward pass.

Among the 1912 graduates was Clarence Page. After seeing an airplane for the first time in 1910, Page turned his attention to aviation and became a legend. He operated flying schools during World War II and founded the Oklahoma Air and Space Museum. An airport west of Oklahoma City bears his name.

An outstanding member of the graduating class of 1913 was Harvey P. Everest, later a successful businessman and banker who flew airplanes with Charles Lindbergh and played bridge with President Lyndon B. Johnson. Everest founded Goodwill of Oklahoma and was a founder of the Oklahoma Medical Research Foundation.

The English and drama programs at the high school helped develop the skills of 1914 graduate Rex Harlow, part of a family of authors and publishers. Harlow edited *Harlow's Weekly*, a leading Oklahoma newspaper of the day, and became a public relations expert and college professor. The author of 75 books, he co-founded the Public Relations Society of America which presents the Rex Harlow Award annually

Harvey P. Everest, Class of 1913.

as its highest honor. Harlow was an adviser to Presidents Herbert Hoover and Franklin D. Roosevelt and made a leading university's list as one of the 12 most influential public relations experts of the twentieth century.

Morrison B. Cunningham, Class of 1916, was Oklahoma City water superintendent for many years and was an internationally famous water quality expert. In 1917, Albert Dyer graduated and went to work in the County Treasurer's office. Later he served four terms as County Treasurer in Oklahoma County.

Other early graduates achieved great success. Stephen S. Chandler graduated from high school in record time while holding down a full-time job at the Rothschild's clothing store. He was appointed federal judge by President Roosevelt in 1940 and served in the position for more than 40 years. Speaking before a U.S. Senate subcommittee in 1970, Chandler gave his own views of a trial judge's burden. His comments were recorded in a 1974 book, *The Benchwarmers*. A trial judge "is driving a 20-mule team down a perilous and hazardous road with precipices on each side, with crafty lawyers often trying to inject error into the record," Chandler said.

During World War I, the size of graduating classes was affected by young men leaving school early to join the fight for freedom overseas. An example was 16-year-old Gerald Clayton who lied about his age and joined the Oklahoma National Guard. His parents thought he was too young to fight and successfully won his discharge. However, young Clayton again lied to regular U.S. Army recruiters and headed to France where he served as an anti-aircraft gunner. Many students returned from military service and reentered high school.

In addition to academic and athletic success, students in other areas of learning were given substantial opportunity at the high school. In the spring of 1917, students presented the light operatic production, "The Mikado." Art students painted scenery and the home economics class made the costumes and draperies. The students of the manual training class built sets. Members of the boys' and girls' glee clubs sang in the chorus, and the school orchestra, conducted by Miss Roberta Worley, provided the music.

In 1917 and 1918, the Oklahoma High School football team won back-to-back state championships. As part of their recognition, Oklahoma City Postmaster Claude Weaver hired all 40 members of the squad to work at the post office to handle the extraordinary volume of packages during the Christmas season.

Oklahoma High basketball players also excelled. In February 1918, the high school team beat the freshman team of the University of Oklahoma after handily defeating other schools in the central Oklahoma high school conference. A 1918 newspaper story noted that the high school also was developing excellent teams in baseball, track, and tennis in preparation for statewide competition.

Oklahoma High School continued to produce star students. In the Class of 1918 was Charles A. Vose, later a legend in Oklahoma banking circles. A fellow student, John Douglas, was one of four first place winners in a national War Savings Bond Stamp poster contest. The local high school was chosen as the first school in the nation to host a month-long exhibit of the winning posters.

The exhibit was brought to Oklahoma City through the efforts of high school art department director, Miss Estelle Manon.

Also in 1918, Bess Mills was the first female to complete the mechanical drawing course at the high school. She later was chief engineer of the Gulf, Colorado and Santa Fe Railroad.

U.S. District Judge Stephen S. Chandler.

3 THE "CENTRAL" HIGH SCHOOL

Even though today all graduates of the high school that served the city for more than 60 years are called graduates of Central High School, Oklahoma City High School was the official name for the school some called "Oklahoma High School" or simply "the high school."

One of the earliest references to "central high school" appeared in an editorial in *The Daily Oklahoman* on February 6, 1919. The editorial, supporting an approaching vote on a bond issue, was a blanket indictment of the crowded conditions in Oklahoma City public schools:

> It is nothing short of an outrage that children should be housed in basement rooms, in wretched frame annexes, and in old firetrap buildings. If we should have a fire in one of these buildings and defenseless children lost their lives, this city would go into mourning…Let us not wait until some terrible tragedy happens. Let us prevent it.

The editorial noted that even with the old Irving Building on Military Hill renovated to house the commercial department of the high school, "There will be left at the Central high school 2,000 students when the building properly can accommodate only 1,300." Even though it would be another seven years before other high schools were built, newspaper writers and civic leaders began referring to Oklahoma High School as "Central High School."

The editorial writers at the newspaper were upset with the apathy among school patrons. Junior high schools were becoming commonplace across the country and Oklahoma City school officials wanted to build several junior highs to take pressure off the overcrowded high school. Beginning in 1916, voters rejected bond issues for building junior high buildings. However, at the urging of the school administration and the newspaper, a $1 million bond issue was passed in 1919, providing for the construction of three new junior high schools, Webster, Capitol Hill, and Classen. All three junior highs opened the following year.

Two interesting developments at the high school were announced in 1919. The City Sunday School Association provided unsalaried Bible teachers to instruct students in an elective Bible history class. The class, which was officially credited to a student's transcript, attracted more than 200 students. The first permanent Oklahoma High School Alumni Association was formed at a meeting of 200 graduates in December 1919. Otis Thompson, Class of 1914, was elected as the first president.

In 1920, A.S. "Mike" Monroney graduated near the top of the class. He later became one of the most powerful members of the U.S. Senate. As a champion of aviation, he was able to bring

Central graduate U.S. Senator A.S. "Mike" Monroney, left, and President John F. Kennedy. *Courtesy Western History Collections, University of Oklahoma Libraries.*

the nation's aeronautical center to his home state. With nearly 6,000 federal employees, the Mike Monroney Aeronautical Center is the U.S. Department of Transportation's largest facility outside Washington, D.C.

In the early 1920s, *The Daily Oklahoman* regularly began referring to Oklahoma City's only high school as "Central high school." In 1922, the school newspaper began using "Central High School" in its masthead.

In 1921, the graduating class skyrocketed to 351, 50 students more than any class before. The commencement address was made by University of Oklahoma President Stratton D. Brooks, who told the students, "I hope that you will not consider that you have reached the pinnacle of accomplishment, but that you will continue to go forward with a broader conception of life and the

Attorney Phil Daugherty was one of the outstanding Central graduates of the 1920s. *Courtesy Oklahoma Historical Society.*

determination to merit the service that has been done for you."

Throughout the 1920s, the physical plant at the high school remained unchanged. The football team played on the Oklahoma City University field, and the high school auditorium was frequently the site of plays and concerts. Jenkins Music Company provided pianos for use by students and often arranged concerts at the auditorium.

Outstanding graduates of the 1920s included businessman, Ed Overholser; famous pianist, Nella Miller; publisher Dan Hogan, Jr.; Dr. George Bozalis; District Judge A.P. Van Meter; attorneys H.K. Berry, Jr., John W. Mee, Phil Daugherty, Charles Schwoerke, Merton Bulla, Frank and George Miskovsky, and Byron McFall; and John Soergel, an All-State player in three

CENTRAL'S GREATEST ATHLETE ???

Alumni can generate valid arguments over who was Central High School's greatest athlete, but most settle on Tom Churchill, senior class president in 1926. He lettered in five sports at Central and was All-American in three sports at the University of Oklahoma. In 1928, he was the first OU athlete to compete in the Olympics. He signed with the New York Yankees, but a shoulder injury kept him in the minor leagues. He later was men's head basketball coach at the University of New Mexico.

Churchill posed for the mural near the Robinson Avenue entrance of the high school building. In 2004, he was inducted into the Oklahoma Sports Hall of Fame, joining two other Central graduates, Bruce Drake and Paul Hansen.

Central's greatest all-around athlete, Tom Churchill. *Courtesy Jim Thorpe Association.*

sports who was considered by some as the capital city's finest all-around athlete of the 1920s.

Other graduates of the decade included William "Skinny" Johnson, an All-American basketball player at the University of Kansas, and one of six brothers to graduate from the high school; Coca Cola bottling executive Henry Browne; Dr. Joseph Messenbaugh; advertising agency owner Lowe Runkle; and John E. Kirkpatrick.

Kirkpatrick, who graduated from the U.S. Naval Academy and ultimately reached the rank of admiral in the U.S. Naval Reserve, left large footprints on Oklahoma during the next half century. His success in the oil business allowed him and his wife, Eleanor, to contribute millions of dollars to many civic and community projects. He established the Oklahoma City Community Foundation.

Academically, Frank Lamb and Catherine McKinney won the Central Oklahoma Conference reading contest in 1921. It was the first time that both the men's and women's divisions had been won by students from the same high school. A Public Night School offered a variety of classes from psychology, French, and shorthand, to cooking, electricity, and cabinet making. The radio department built a 100-watt amateur radio transmitter. The instrumental and vocal music programs presented spring and fall concerts, much to the delight of the growing population of the capital city.

John E. Kirkpatrick *Courtesy Oklahoma Hall of Fame.*

High school athletes were excited about a 1922 announcement that Central High may become the first high school in the nation to have its own standard-sized athletic stadium. Principal C.W. Gethmann proposed that the city give the school district an abandoned brick pit at Northwest Fifteenth Street and McKinley Avenue. Gethmann theorized that seats could be built on the sloping sides of the brick pit at little cost. Local baseball teams had been playing on the surface of the pit for the previous two years. Even though school officials and patrons were high on the proposal, the city council failed to act upon it and the baseball team continued to play at the Western League Ball Park and the football Cardinals played at the OCU Field.

Athletic teams flourished. The football team dominated surrounding teams such as El Reno and Edmond. Ed Overholser was the top tennis player in 1925. Cardinal baseball, basketball, and golf teams competed well against other high schools in central Oklahoma.

Bruce Drake was a Central basketball star and continued his excellent play as an All-American at the University of Oklahoma after he graduated from high school in 1924. He was head men's basketball coach at OU from 1938 to 1955 and is a member of the National Basketball Hall of Fame.

Success in athletics sometimes brings intense scrutiny. That occurred with Central in 1925 when the high school had to defend charges made by the Oklahoma High School Athletic Association that two players were ineligible for two very different reasons. Charges that football star Elias Funk had been paid to play baseball the previous summer, and therefore was ineligible for high school play as a professional, were dropped because of insufficient evidence. However, the Cardinals had to forfeit all football games in which Red Bonner had played the previous season. State school officials found that Bonner had not been truthful when he signed an affidavit that he lived in the Oklahoma City school district.

Mary Gray Thompson began teaching speech or oratory at Central in 1922. For the next 15 years she trained outstanding public speakers such as Congressman John Jarman, State Senator George Miskovsky, Tom Paxton of WKY Radio and Television, Radio Free Europe announcer Dave Soureek, Voice of America announcer Russel Black, and Eugene Sanders and Amzie Strickland, both stars of radio drama series in New York City.

In 1925, plans were announced to build a Physical Education Annex on the west side of the original building on lots where an old house stood. Once the house was removed, construction

Ed Overholser was Oklahoma City's 16th mayor. *Courtesy Oklahoma Historical Society.*

Central basketball star Bruce Drake is a member of the National Basketball Hall of Fame. *Courtesy Jim Thorpe Association.*

began and was completed in 1928.

Oklahoma High School officially became Central High School in 1926 when Classen Junior High School was converted to Classen High School. Two years later, Capitol Hill High School was built. Both schools served students who lived far from Central High School location at Northwest Seventh and Robinson. In 1930, Central graduated only 382 students, down 40 percent from five years previous. The two other high schools had relieved enrollment pressure from Central. The same year, Classen's graduating class numbered 403 and Capitol Hill graduated 159.

A 1930 postcard of Central High School. *Courtesy Oklahoma Historical Society.*

Central High School was known for training students for skilled jobs in the community. *Courtesy Oklahoma Historical Society.*

A GROWING CAMPUS

After the Physical Education Annex was completed in 1928, additional buildings were added to the campus. The former Orange Inn, just west of the P.E. Annex, was converted into the carpentry shop. A former apartment complex at Northwest Eighth and Harvey became the Inverness Boyd Museum and Institute of Art. In 1949, the Seventh Day Adventist church was bought by the School Board and converted into the Central cosmetology and barbering facility. In 1951, a General Vocational building was constructed and used for sheet metal repair, cabinetry, and other vocational classes, and a building at 815 North Harvey was purchased to house automobile repair classes.

The 1928 Central High School Brass Band still carried the drum used by Oklahoma City High School. *Courtesy Oklahoma Historical Society.*

4 CONTINUED EXCELLENCE

Although enrollment was down at Central in the 1930s, the school continued to be the location of choice for many civic club meetings and community concerts. Extension classes from the University of Oklahoma were offered and the school began offering more technical and trade classes. Central students fared well in debate and music competitions. A 100-piece band was unveiled in 1931.

The innovative administration created summer music courses at the high school, and creative students in the trade classes built an airplane. The interest in flying and the establishment of a high school flying club was encouraged by local aviator Johnny Burke, manager of

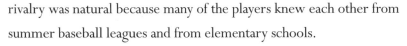

the Wiley Post Airplane Company. Wiley Post lived in Oklahoma City and visited with Central students between his pioneer flights around the world.

In athletics, the Central-Classen rivalry grew with each passing season in football, baseball, track, and basketball. The

rivalry was natural because many of the players knew each other from summer baseball leagues and from elementary schools.

The 1930s produced several extraordinary graduates from Central High School, especially in the field of public service. In a three-year span from 1930 to 1932, a famous federal judge, a state prosecutor, a congressman, and presidential adviser received their Central diplomas. In 1930, future Oklahoma County County Attorney Granville Tomerlin, automobile magnate Ralph Bolen, and future Oklahoma City mayor and Oklahoma Historical Society president George Shirk graduated. Shirk was one of three mayors of Oklahoma City who graduated from Central; the others were Ed Overholser and Allen Street.

In 1931, John Jarman, a longtime congressman from Oklahoma's First Congressional District, and future commanding general of the 45th Infantry Division and federal judge, Fred Daugherty, were among the top seniors. In 1932,

Central High School graduate Victor Holt, Jr., served as president of the Goodyear Tire & Rubber Company in Akron, Ohio, in the 1950s. *Courtesy University of Akron.*

Allen Street, a graduate of Central High, was mayor of Oklahoma City for 12 years in the 1940s and 1950s. Earlier he served five terms in the Oklahoma House of Representatives and was Speaker of the House in 1928.

Bryce Harlow graduated from Central at age 15 and entered college at the University of Oklahoma. He later served as a cabinet-level adviser to three presidents. Former President Gerald Ford said Harlow knew more about Congress than any presidential adviser in history.

Another public servant, Jack Cornett, a longtime member of the city council in Oklahoma City, graduated in 1937. Other outstanding graduates of the 1930s included attorney James Linn, businessman Joe Sears, and Dr. Henry Freede, Jr. Freede was trained as an orthopedic surgeon and performed the world's first quadruple amputation at a U.S. Army field hospital on Guam during World War II.

Several Central graduates of the decade were radio, television, and stage performers. Amzie Strickland played the lead role on several network radio serials and made more than 600 television appearances in shows such as *Gunsmoke*, *The Andy Griffith Show*, *I Love Lucy*, *Bonanza*, *Perry Mason*, and *The Twilight Zone*. She also appeared in a half-dozen movies, including *Shiloh* and *Pretty Woman*. Margaret Ledbetter, under the stage name Margaret Garland, was a champion orator at Central and then appeared as Dr. Joan Dale in *Tom Corbett, Space Cadet* on radio and in the early days of television.

Charles Carshon was national champion in dramatic declaration in 1937 and 1938 while a student at Central and later starred with Imogene

George Shirk. *Courtesy Oklahoma Historical Society.*

Congressman John Jarman, Class of 1931. *Courtesy Oklahoma Historical Society.*

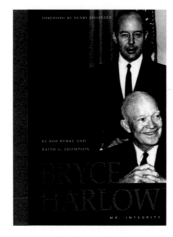

Coco in *Happy Birthday* and played in the famous Broadway production of *Billy Bud*. Russel Black was national oratorical champion in 1935 and, after working in radio at WNAD in Norman and WKY in Oklahoma City, left for Washington, D.C., for a long career as an announcer and producer for the Voice of America. Bill Canfield, a champion public speaker at Central, appeared on the television crime film series, *Treasury Men in Action*, and narrated many commercial films.

As had occurred during World War I, many young high school men at Central dropped out of classes and joined the military to fight on distant battlefields in World War II. At home, the University of Oklahoma used classrooms at Central to teach tuition-free day and night classes to help with the war effort. Classes included welding, engineering fundamentals, and engineering drawing. The training was tied to the need for skilled workers at the Douglas Aircraft Company plant in Midwest City. The plant built more than half the 10,000 C-47 U.S. Army "Gooney Bird" cargo planes used in World War II. Often, students at Central were hired on the spot during training and processed for employment at the defense plant.

At the end of the war, nearly 70 former Central

Central graduate Bryce Harlow was one of the most respected presidential advisers in the nation's capital for a generation. He was the subject of a 2002 biography published by the Oklahoma Hall of Fame.

Central High graduate Fred Daugherty commanded the 45th Infantry Division and was appointed federal judge by President John F. Kennedy. *Courtesy Oklahoma Historical Society.*

Central alumnus Dr. Henry Freede, Jr., was the subject of a 2009 biography. *Courtesy Oklahoma Hall of Fame.*

graduates and students, and one instructor, L.H. Showalter, were honored for giving the supreme sacrifice of their life in the conflict.

Several prominent professional athletes and college coaches graduated from Central during the 1940s. Ellis F. "Cot" Deal, Class of 1941, spent 48 years in baseball as a player, manager, coach, and executive. He pitched for the Boston Red Sox and St. Louis Cardinals in the major leagues for four seasons, was a major league pitching coach for several teams, and managed two minor league teams, including the Oklahoma City 89ers. Deal died in Oklahoma City in 2013 at the age of 90.

Also in the Class of 1941 was Harold W. "Hal" Lahar. After military service in the South Pacific, Lahar played football at the University of Oklahoma and spent three years in the National Football League with the Chicago Bears and Buffalo Bills. His greatest contribution to sports was as head football coach at Colgate University for 11 seasons and at the University of Houston for five years.

Dee Andros came from a Greek immigrant family, was an All-State tackle under Coach Dale Arbuckle, and graduated from Central in 1941. He joined the U.S. Marine Corps the following year and saw action in the Pacific. He was present at the historic moment when Marines raised the American flag on Iwo Jima. Andros returned to Oklahoma and played guard for Coach Bud Wilkinson at the University of Oklahoma. After serving as an assistant football coach at OU and other NCAA schools, he became the head coach at the University of Idaho before finding a home at Oregon State University, where he was football coach for 11 years and athletic director for another 11 years.

An outstanding major league pitching star from Central was

Actress Amzie Strickland graduated from Central High School. She appeared in many television sitcoms such as *The Andy Griffith Show. Courtesy Oklahoma Historical Society.*

Central graduate Cot Deal left a huge imprint on baseball in America. *Courtesy Topps Inc.*

Dee Andros was a Cardinal football hero and successful college football coach. *Courtesy Oklahoma Historical Society.*

Central baseball hurler Cal McLish had the longest legal name in major league baseball history. *Courtesy Topps Inc.*

Paul Hansen. *Courtesy Jim Thorpe Association.*

Legendary running back Buck McPhail graduated from Central. *Courtesy University of Oklahoma.*

Cal McLish whose legal name was the longest in major league baseball history. His father was given the chance to name his son. In honor of the father's heroes and the capital of the Choctaw Nation, the baby boy was named Calvin Coolidge Julius Caesar Tuskahoma McLish. He pitched in the major leagues for 15 seasons with seven teams, including the Brooklyn Dodgers and Pittsburgh Pirates. When McLish shut out the Capitol Hill Redskins during his senior year in 1943, the newspaper reporter called him a "fiery Central highschool hurler."

In 1947, Paul Hansen, later one of Oklahoma's most beloved basketball coaches, graduated from Central. He was head men's basketball coach at Oklahoma State University, Oklahoma City University, and the University of Science and Arts of Oklahoma. Based upon his 40 years of coaching experience, he was inducted into the Oklahoma Sports Hall of Fame.

Coleman "Buck" McPhail graduated from Central in 1949. Called one of the greatest Oklahoma high school running backs in history, McPhail and Billy Vessels won All-American honors in 1952 at the University of Oklahoma where they became the first two backs on a collegiate football team to each gain 1,000 rushing yards in the same season. McPhail played two seasons for the Baltimore Colts of the National Football League and later coached football at the University of California and the University of Illinois.

The annual football war between Central and Classen often produced pre-game battles between students. In 1946, the newspaper headline was "Central Wins on Gridiron; Police Lose Pregame Battle." Eight students were arrested on charges of disorderly conduct and egg-splattered police officers declared they wanted no more of the "so-called frivolity" between the two rivals. After the arrests, School Superintendent Dr. H.B. Bruner considered calling off the game, but decided not to penalize the "great mass of students" who acted with good manners and stayed far from the egg and rotten tomato throwing.

A similar incident occurred in 1949, although the trouble came after the Central-Classen football game.

Hal Lahar was a longtime collegiate football coach. *Courtesy Jim Thorpe Association.*

A large crowd gathered downtown at Main Street and Robinson Avenue. Traffic was tied up for 45 minutes because windshields of cars were covered with eggs thrown from students hiding in the crowd. No arrests were made.

By the early 1950s, there were seven high schools in Oklahoma City. Central, Classen, and Capitol Hill were joined by Northeast High School, John Marshall High School, Southeast High School, and Douglass High School. As residents built homes farther from downtown, it was necessary for even more high schools to be placed on the drawing board of school planners. Within a few years, U.S. Grant High School and Northwest Classen High School were added.

Lou Antonio, right, Class of 1952, performed in several Broadway productions but spent most of his acting and directing career in Hollywood. He appeared in television shows such as *Gunsmoke, Mission: Impossible, Star Trek,* and *I Dream of Jeannie.* Moving behind the camera, he directed several television movies and episodes of television series such as *The Rockford Files, The West Wing,* and *CSI: Crime Scene Investigation. Courtesy Oklahoma Publishing Company.*

Central graduate Don Chastain became a prominent actor on Broadway and in Hollywood. *Courtesy Oklahoma Publishing Company.*

As a result of decaying neighborhoods, families moving to the suburbs, and a smaller area from which to draw students, Central's enrollment grew stale in the 1950s. The startling growth enjoyed in the school's first 40 years was now but a note in history. In 1953, the senior class at Central numbered 370 compared to 472 at Classen, 453 at Capitol Hill, 143 at Douglass, 135 at Northeast, 87 at Southeast, and 73 at John Marshall.

To make good use of the aging Central High School building, hundreds of adults enrolled each semester in the Adult Institute. The novel program offered practical subjects such as bookkeeping, business law, body and fender repair, drafting, auto mechanics, and slide rule usage. In addition to job skills classes, courses such as ceramics, art, tailoring, and fishing fly tying were offered in the hobby and self-improvement category.

Don Chastain, Class of 1953, starred in Central drama productions and then headed to New York City and Hollywood after college. He appeared in several Broadway plays, including a lead role in *No Strings, Superman,* and *42nd Street.* He was Debbie Reynolds' husband in television's *The Debbie Reynolds Show,* and was a guest star in television shows such as *Hawaii-Five-O, Scrubs, The Rockford Files, All My Children,* and *The West Wing.*

In 1954, Oklahoma City schools remained

segregated between whites and blacks. Oklahoma was one of 17 southern states that retained laws that mandated the races be segregated for educational purposes. Against that backdrop, the U.S. Supreme Court in *Brown v. Board of Education* decided that separate schools were inherently unequal and began the tedious process of deciding how the nation's schools would be integrated.

On August 1, 1955, the Oklahoma City School Board unanimously voted to fully integrate the city's public schools. The board's action wiped out the old system of separate schools superimposed on the racial makeup of the city and created neighborhood schools. School Superintendent Dr. J. Chester Swanson said, "We are not going to keep a child from going to the school within the natural boundaries where he lives."

The integration of Central High in September 1955 occurred with relative ease as black students from the Lincoln and Culbertson areas and neighborhoods west of the Santa Fe Railroad enrolled. Central was the first of the Oklahoma City high schools to fully integrate.

Central continued to field competitive teams in several sports. All-State catcher Mike Brumley, Class of 1956, later played three seasons for the major league Washington Senators. After baseball, he became a well-known Baptist minister in Florida. His son, also named Mike Brumley, played for several major league teams for a dozen seasons and was first base coach for the Seattle Mariners in 2013.

The debating society at Central celebrated its 54th year in 1959 and held a banquet at O'Mealey's Cafeteria for Miss Eva Chowning, the school librarian for 35 years, to honor her sponsorship of the Jeffersonian Debating Society for more than three decades.

The *Cardinal* yearbook in 1957 noted the 50th anniversary of Oklahoma. *Courtesy Central High School Alumni Association.*

5 YEARS OF TRANSITION

In July, 1962, U.S. District Judge Luther Bohanon ordered the Oklahoma City School Board to formulate a plan to fully integrate the city's public schools. The federal judge ruled that only "token" integration had occurred since the U.S. Supreme Court edict in *Brown v. Board of Education* eight years before.

The following year, the School Board submitted a comprehensive plan to integrate both students and faculty. However, Judge Bohanon turned down the plan and a legal fight ensued for many years.

Central High School had two problems. The building was now more than a half century old and needed substantial repairs and renovation. The second problem was declining enrollment. Central had the lowest student to teacher ratio in the Oklahoma City district at 26.3 students per teacher, compared with 32 students per teacher at Taft Junior High School.

In 1966, the School Board submitted yet another plan that combined the attendance districts of Central and Classen high schools, but would make one of them a junior high school. Because of the dwindling student enrollment at Central, school officials kept Classen open as a high school and relegated Central to become a junior high school at the end of the 1967-1968 school year.

It was the end of an era at commencement exercises on May 29, 1968, when the last graduating class of Central walked across the stage. There were only 133 seniors, compared to 705 seniors at Northwest Classen and 670 at U.S. Grant. Joseph Mays, a 1954 Central graduate and a reporter for *The Daily Oklahoman*, wrote about the final commencement:

Ceiling fans creaked and onlookers used programs as hand fans in a vain attempt to cut the summer heat in the 59-year-old auditorium. Next fall, the school will become a junior high under a federal plan seeking integration. Ironically, the appearance of the 133 graduates was proof Central already is integrated. About one-third of the graduates were Negro.

Longtime speech teacher Maybelle Conger, a 1924 graduate, introduced the commencement speaker, Principal Joe Lawter. A 1939 graduate, Lawter assumed the principal's job eight years before. He noted that more than 600 Central graduates had earned doctorate degrees. Lawter said about the heavily racially mixed class, "These people have learned to live with each other. We should learn by their example. We all need to learn to live together." School Superintendent Dr. Bill Lillard presented diplomas and said, "Central, with the spirit and tradition it has, will always live." After its transition to a junior high, high school students at Central were transferred to Classen.

Not only was it an end of an era in the classroom for Central, under a sports page headline, "Death of Central Cards Closes City Football Era," in August, 1968, Lynn Garnand traced the history of Oklahoma and Central High School athletics, including an 1895 game football game against Guthrie, the first high school game in the history of the future state. That same year, the University of Oklahoma introduced football and the Cardinals beat the OU team 34-6. Garnand wrote, "Central has fielded a team every year since 1895, some of them very good, including mythical state champions in 1906, 1914, 1917, 1918, 1919, 1938, and 1939."

Even though it officially ended training high school students, Central graduates continued to excel. In 1968, Harold J. Sullivan was named executive director of the Oklahoma Bar Association after serving 23 years in the U.S. Air Force, rising to the rank of colonel. Ted Foster was named dean of the Oklahoma City University School of Law in 1969. Speech teacher Maybelle Conger appeared in newspaper advertisements for Classen Alumnus Barry Albert's campaign for the Oklahoma House of Representatives. In the ad, Conger called Albert a "square," in the best sense, "He believes in making everyone a SQUARE DEAL." Albert also served as Secretary of the Oklahoma County Election Board.

The first class to hold a reunion after Central High School had faded into history was the Class of 1949 for their 20-year reunion in the summer of 1969. Among the notable graduates who attended the reunion were State Senator Cleeta John Rogers, former OU running great Buck McPhail, and U.S. Army Lieutenant Colonel Howard Stone.

After several years as a junior high school, Central became, technically, a high school again as the Central Innovative High School in 1976. Principal Bob Alyea described the new program as one which

John McCormick was one of the rare students who graduated both from Central High School and the Oklahoma City University School of Law. He attended Central from 1961 to 1965 and graduated from OCU Law in 1979. He was a judge of the Oklahoma Workers' Compensation Court and general counsel of CompSource Mutual Insurance Company.

Central High School students cheer the signboard they erected near the school backing their Capital Conference champion Cardinals in November, 1966. *Courtesy Oklahoma Publishing Company Photography Collection, Oklahoma Historical Society.*

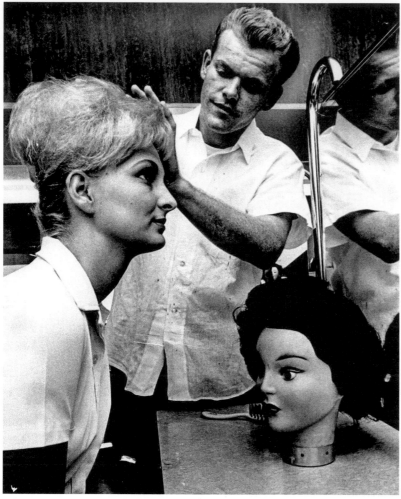

Mickey Hill was one of the nation's first male cosmetology students at Central in 1968 in a program funded by the Manpower Training Act. Courtesy *Oklahoma Publishing Company Photography Collection, Oklahoma Historical Society.*

could give the bright accelerated student and the apathetic possible dropout the kind of individual education each needed. A lottery provided the 222 students for the Central program which allowed students to spend part of their day in the classroom and several hours working in the community. School officials defended the new Innovative High School by trumpeting the success of similar programs in other states and the opportunity to experiment with new teaching and counseling methods.

When the school district decided to move the Innovative High School, Central High School was put on the market in 1981. Many businesses and organizations expressed interest in the 71-year-old building that had been added to the National Register of Historic Places in 1975. The successful bidder was Southwestern Bell Telephone Company. During the next three years, the company spent $12 million to renovate the interior and exterior of the building which was renamed "One Bell Central." The renovation included a central atrium, skylights, glass elevators, and a museum to house Central High School records and memorabilia. The museum was dedicated during the All-Class reunion in 1984.

For past students and alumni, the establishment of the museum was a special occasion. In addition to sports and academic trophies, letter jackets, yearbooks, pep club uniforms, rows of seats, photographs, and an original display included a bust of Mary Couch, the school's first teacher, were donated.

The renewed interest in the Alumni Association resulted in a 1983 revival of *Sooner Spirit*, the school newspaper that had ceased publication when the high school closed. The renewal of the means of communication with alumni was the idea of Hallie Collins, the first president of the newly-formed Alumni Association, and Charles Able.

The Southwestern Bell renovation also included removal of a 1928 addition to the gymnasium and many of the vocational shops added to the original building in the 1940s. Also removed was a skywalk. Each of the building's 360 windows had to be replaced to meet new building standards.

The excellence of the renovation of the building was recognized with honors from the American Institute of Architects and American Society of Interior Designers. The refurbished exterior and interior were featured in national design publications.

Alumni honored two Central High graduates in 1984 as the first winners of the Central High School Alumni Association Distinguished Alumni Award. Dr. Charles Hugh Wilson, a professor of surgery at the University of Oklahoma College of Medicine and author of many medical journal articles, and Jack R. Durland, former president of Cain's Coffee Company, were the two recipients.

In 1992, Central High alumni marked the centennial of the high school. Alumni Association president Frances Percival and his army of volunteers painstakingly searched for contact information for many of the 22,000 students who had passed through the halls of the school for most of the twentieth century. More than 2,000 students enjoyed visiting with old friends during the three day event.

The Central High Museum was damaged when a truck bomb exploded on the morning of April 19, 1995, in front of the Alfred P. Murrah Federal Building in downtown Oklahoma City, two blocks south of the school. Alumni Association president Vernon Forshee drove to the Southwestern Bell building and discovered broken glass display cases in the museum. The blast shook marble from the walls. Southwestern Bell graciously paid for the repairs.

Maybelle Conger was honored in 1979 for teaching speech at Central for 34 years. *Courtesy Oklahoma Publishing Company Photography Collection, Oklahoma Historical Society.*

Vice Admiral Edward Tidd, Class of 1943, served 33 years in the U.S. Navy and was commander of Naval Surface Force of the U.S. Pacific Fleet. *Courtesy U.S. Navy.*

Dancer and dramatist Margaret Snow, third from left, directs students in a dance workshop at Central Innovative High School in 1981. *Courtesy Oklahoma Publishing Company Photography Collection, Oklahoma Historical Society.*

Nostalgia and history merged each time Central High alumni met. *Courtesy Oklahoma Publishing Company Photography Collection, Oklahoma Historical Society.*

The old school served a valuable service during the chaos that followed the Murrah Building bombing. The building and its adjacent parking lot served as a staging area for rescue operations as emergency responders looked for survivors and then began the tedious task of recovering the bodies of the 168 men, women, and children killed in the bombing.

In early 2005, Oklahoma Farmers Union Mutual Insurance Company purchased the old Central High Building from AT&T, the successor company to Southwestern Bell, for $8 million. A casualty of the sale was the closing of the Central High Museum. The owners cited liability issues for the action. Frances Percival, president of the Central High School Alumni Association, called the closing of the museum a "crushing blow." He was concerned that alumni would no longer have "ties to our school."

Central alumnus William "Bill" Caudill, standing, was posthumously awarded the highest prize in architecture in 1985. He founded one of world's largest architectural firms in Houston, Texas, and joined the likes of Frank Lloyd Wright and Buckminster Fuller on the short list of winners of the Gold Medal of the American Institute of Architects.

New Life for a Landmark

When Southwestern Bell Telephone Company purchased the building, it was renamed One Bell Central. *Courtesy Oklahoma Historical Society.*

The old high school building in the 1980s. *Courtesy Central High School Alumni Association.*

Inspecting items in the Museum Room in 1985 are, left to right, Frances Stevenson Percival, Class of 1946, Jack Moses, Class of 1944, and Charles Able, Class of 1935. *Courtesy Oklahoma Publishing Company Photography Collection, Oklahoma Historical Society.*

In October 2005, AT&T sponsored a reception that accompanied the closing of the Central High Museum. More than 200 alumni attended the reception at which the Alumni Association honored June Honiker and Imogene and W.O. Nikkel for their long service to the museum. Patti Hobson Hall and Oscar Jackson reminisced about their Central experiences, and Charles Harris led the group in "Hail Alma Mater" and the Central fight song. Don Wood wrote in *Sooner Spirit*, "There was not a dry eye in the house." After the closing of the museum, the artifacts were transferred for safekeeping at the Oklahoma History Center. The Red Skirts, the proud Central pep club from 1930 to 1961, celebrated its 77th anniversary in 2007 at the Skirvin Hotel. One hundred thirty three former Red Skirts attended the celebration. Another 87 former members of the Black Skirts also held a reunion and remembered the

days of the Black Skirt String Band and Choir.

Also in 2007, the new owner of the building changed its name and began talking about selling the "one of a kind" historic site. A broker in charge of marketing the property said, "There is simply no other building like it in Oklahoma City."

In 2012, the 101-year-old Central High School building became the subject of two rivals bidding for the landmark. Oklahoma City Public Schools announced plans to purchase the old high school for use as an administration building.

The other bidder was the Oklahoma City University School of Law. The growing law school had outgrown its facilities on the OCU campus at Northwest 23rd and Blackwelder. Ron Norick, chairman of the OCU Board of Trustees, OCU President Robert Henry, and Law School Dean

Graduates of the 1960s gathered in 2003 for a reunion. *Courtesy Central High School Alumni Association.*

An example of specific class reunions among CHS graduates was the 2004 reunion of graduates of the last decade of the school's existence. *Courtesy Central High School Alumni Association.*

Valerie Couch led the negotiations with the owner of the building.

Oklahoma City University was the winning bidder. A letter of intent to purchase the building was signed by the University on July 16, 2012. In October, the University's Board of Trustees made the purchase official. Learning was returning to the heart of the capital city.

The return of learning to the heart of Oklahoma City surely warmed the memories of the thousands of living students who walked the halls of Central High. Part of their pride in the historic landmark which was their home for high school was best expressed in a 2012 edition of *Sooner Spirit*:

> It's a beautiful place to visit and refresh dreams. And we, the living alumni of Central High School, are mindful of the teachers who made the school a true place of learning. We remember our classmates who studied, laughed, cheered, roamed the halls, participated in all sorts of clubs and activities…and we sing the Fight Song with true reverence when we proclaim Hail Alma Mater!

The registration desk for the 2010 all school reunion. *Courtesy Central High School Alumni Association.*

Oscar Jackson, Class of 1965, who served as Oklahoma Secretary of Human Resources and Administration, has worked to grow scholarship funds donated to the Central High School Alumni Fund. Tied to the Oklahoma City Community Foundation, the endowment has grown significantly in recent years, thanks to the guidance of Jackson, the chair of the Scholarship Committee of the Central High Alumni Association. The funds provide several scholarships each year.

The State of Oklahoma made available a special license plate for Central High School graduates.

6 WHY A DOWNTOWN LAW SCHOOL?

Having the Oklahoma City University School of Law located in rejuvenated downtown Oklahoma City is neither a new idea or unique among American cities and their law schools. In fact, Oklahoma City University School of Law had a strong presence in downtown 80 years ago.

Oklahoma City University School of Law is the state's oldest law school, tracing its roots to the Epworth University School of Law founded in 1907, two months before Oklahoma joined the Union as the 46th state. When Epworth University began classes three years before, leaders believed that a law school was necessary because university graduates who desired a career in law were leaving the state to earn their degrees.

The law school was only the fourth three-year institution of its kind south of the Ohio River as evening classes with 15 students began under the watchful eye of the first dean, C.B. Ames. The purpose of the study regimen was to prepare students for the Oklahoma bar examination. Lecturers at the law school included famous names in Oklahoma City history such as John W. Shartel, owner of the city's trolley system; John H. Burford, the last chief justice of the Oklahoma territorial Supreme Court; and legendary federal judge, Edgar S. Vaught.

Two forces caused the closing of the Epworth law school before its first class could graduate. The university's sponsor, the Methodist churches of Texas and Oklahoma, suffered a rift that depleted funds necessary for the university to continue. The other force was pressure from state officials who wanted the state to have its own law school. Negotiations produced the closure of the Epworth law school, establishment of a state-run school at Norman at the University of Oklahoma, and guaranteed graduation of the Epworth students from OU. The Epworth law school even donated its law library to OU.

Even though the state university was training future lawyers, there remained a strong sentiment in Oklahoma City during the next decade that students should be able to earn a law degree in the capital city. The preference was that any law school in Oklahoma City should be located downtown. In 1925, a private law school, Oklahoma City College of Law, was founded by Roger Stephens. Other proprietary, privately-owned law schools, were established, including the Central Oklahoma Law School, founded by F. Bert Grubb.

In 1933, Oklahoma City University joined forces with Grubb to offer a bachelor of arts program for students enrolled in the Central Oklahoma Law School. Tuition was $7.50 per month. However, the economic downturn that resulted from the Great Depression caused a reduction in students and the joint venture ended. Later, Grubb's school merged with the Oklahoma City College of Law and private legal education continued to grow in Oklahoma City.

The Oklahoma City College of Law was successful partly because of its location—downtown. With its growth in numbers and prestige, the state legislature granted the school authority to award a bachelor of laws degree in 1945. The school's downtown location allowed students who worked in the area to quickly travel to the law school. The College of Law was located in several downtown venues including the Harn Building at 220 Northwest Third Street and the old YMCA building.

The downtown location also allowed the recruitment of women students who worked full-time secretary jobs for lawyers or judges at the nearby federal and state courthouses. Bert Grubb lauded the fact that a dozen women law students were enrolled in 1945. The school pursued women enrollment a quarter century before American women began applying to law school in large numbers. The law school's *Bulletin* boasted, "No longer are the doors of the legal profession closed to her. She is leading her classes…and taking her place alongside the ablest lawyers…"

Even before Oklahoma City University acquired the proprietary Oklahoma City College of Law, the University offered many classes at a downtown location. The 1945 OCU *Bulletin* called OCU "The University Downtown." University officials reasoned that many students could be attracted if classes were offered closer to their jobs.

It was not unusual for Oklahoma City College of Law students to work during the day and attend classes at night. Marian Opala, later Chief Justice of the Oklahoma Supreme Court, worked at a

C.B. Ames, a distinguished member of the Oklahoma bar and judge was the first dean of the law school. *Courtesy, Western History Collections, University of Oklahoma.*

The University Downtown
Fall Semester

OKLAHOMA CITY UNIVERSITY
DOWNTOWN

YMCA

The Doorway Of Opportunity

Oklahoma City University Bulletin
Oklahoma City, Oklahoma

The 1945 *Oklahoma City University Bulletin* announced the presence of OCU downtown.

lumberyard by day and went to school at night. Robert Empie, later Oklahoma Banking Commissioner, was typical of students whose learning had been interrupted by World War II. After his return from the European battlefields, Empie used the G.I. Bill to pay for tuition for law school.

As far back as the 1940s, Oklahoma City University had expressed interest in purchasing the Oklahoma City College of Law and reentering the legal education picture in Oklahoma City. A deal was struck in 1952 and a large "OCU" sign was attached to the outside of the old YMCA building on Northwest Second Street, and six-foot letters, "OCU," were painted on a small structure on top of the building. OCU proudly announced its law school presence in downtown.

Students such as Marian Opala were excited about Oklahoma City University taking over the law school. He said, "Everybody was happy because most of us...knew that the proprietary law school life was a very hazardous enterprise and did not have much prospect of surviving." The University kept Bert Grubb and Roger Stephens on the law school faculty, and Stephens served as the first dean of the Oklahoma City University School of Law. The university purchased the YMCA building for $300,000 and spent another $50,000 on furniture and renovation.

The first Oklahoma City University School of Law class graduated in spring of 1953. Opala and his best friend, George Sam Caporal, were among the graduates. At an alumni meeting, former graduates of the Oklahoma City College of Law decided to be called OCU alumni. There was no objection when Governor Johnston Murray, who previously graduated from the Oklahoma City College of Law and was an active member of the alumni association, referred

The Oklahoma City University School of Law began classes in the old downtown YMCA Building in 1952.

to himself as an Oklahoma City University School of Law alumnus.

In 1956, Oklahoma City University School of Law moved from downtown to the OCU campus at Northwest 23rd and Blackwelder. For classroom space, law students shared the newly-constructed Gold Star Building with students from the school of religion and other liberal arts departments. Dean John G. Hervey increased the prestige and standards of the law school. In 1959, Dean Hervey moved the law school to former World War II barracks on the north side of the campus. It was part of a master plan to expand classroom space and secure accreditation from the American Bar Association.

In the 1970s, Dean Ted Foster was a visionary leader. He opened a day division of classes and began to recruit and hire faculty nationwide. A renovated Gold Star Building became the new home of the law school in 1979 and housed classrooms and faculty and administration offices until the Sarkeys Law Center opened in 1994. Even after the move into the new building, the law library and faculty offices remained in the Gold Star Building.

The final decade of the twentieth century and the first decade of the present century have been a time of maturation for the School of Law. Membership in the Association of American Law Schools came in 2003 as scholarships and enrollment increased. The prestige of the graduates also grew. In 1978, no graduate of the law school had ever served on the Oklahoma Supreme Court. By 2010, three graduates, Marian Opala, Yvonne Kauger, and James Winchester were members of the high court. In 2011, graduate Douglas Combs became a member of the Supreme Court.

In 2012, Valerie Couch became the first woman and former federal judge to be named dean of Oklahoma City University

Marian Opala was the first Oklahoma City University Law graduate appointed to the Oklahoma Supreme Court. *Courtesy Oklahoma Hall of Fame.*

For nearly six decades the Gold Star Building on the OCU campus has been home to certain functions of the law school.

Sarkeys Law Center became the principal home of Oklahoma City University School of Law in 1994.

Law School Dean Ted Foster, right, congratulates law student Mrs. R.L. Sifford, the wife of a heart specialist, who drove three times each week from Wichita, Kansas, to attend classes. *Courtesy Oklahoma Historical Socity.*

Yvonne Kauger, '69, has been a justice of the Oklahoma Supreme Court since 1984. She was the driving force behind the spectacular renovation of the Wiley Post Building into the Oklahoma Judicial Center. Justice Kauger personally selected 70 pieces of art on display in the Judicial Center. *Courtesy Oklahoma Publishing Company.*

School of Law. With the help of prominent alumni and OCU President Robert Henry, Dean Couch looked toward downtown with the vision that the law school should return to where it existed when the Oklahoma City College of Law was acquired in 1952, 60 years before.

Dean Couch saw the purchase of the old Central High School building as a grand opportunity to provide a unique level of access to the legal profession, for both students and those served by the Law School's clinics and experiential programs. The closeness to the county and federal courthouses and thousands of private law offices is unequaled in Oklahoma. On the other hand, legal professionals will find helpful the close proximity to Oklahoma City University School of Law students, faculty, and librarians. Access to the expertise of the faculty and law librarians is invaluable for attorneys dealing with novel and complex subjects.

Many of the major law schools in the nation are located in the downtown area of their cities. These include law schools at Georgetown University, Loyola of Los Angeles, the University of Nevada at Las Vegas, Northwestern University, and Loyola of Chicago. In fact, since the start of the 21st century, a trend has developed toward law schools leaving their main campuses and relocating downtown. Examples are Arizona State University, St. Louis University, and the University of Memphis.

Many other prestigious law schools offer classes in a downtown location of their cities. These include the University of Chicago, Columbia University, University of Houston, George Washington University, University of Pennsylvania, Boston University, Marquette University, University of Denver, DePaul University, Georgia State

James Winchester, '77, was appointed as a justice of the Oklahoma Supreme Court in 2000.

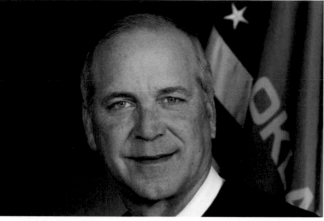

Douglas Combs, '76, was appointed to the Oklahoma Supreme Court in 2011 and served as Chief Justice from 2017–2019.

Todd Lamb, '05, served as Lieutenant Governor of Oklahoma. *Courtesy Oklahoma Publishing Company.*

Mickey Edwards, '69, receiving an Honorary Doctor of Juridical Science from Interim Dean Lee Peoples at the school's 2018 graduation ceremony. Edwards served as a member of the United States House of Representatives from Oklahoma from 1977 to 1993 and was a professor and lecturer at major American universities such as Harvard's Kennedy School of Government and Princeton University.

Ernest Istook, '76, served seven terms in the United States House of Representatives, representing Oklahoma's Fifth District from 1993 to 2007. *Courtesy Oklahoma Publishing Company.*

Enoch Kelly Haney, '64, served in the Oklahoma State Senate and was Principal Chief of the Seminole Nation of Oklahoma. He sculpted *The Guardian* that adorns the top of the dome of the Oklahoma State Capitol.

David Holt, '09, served in the Oklahoma State Senate and was elected Mayor of Oklahoma City in 2018.

Members of the Class of 2017 gather at their new law school. *Courtesy Ann Sherman.*

University, and Fordham University.

For more than a century, Oklahoma City University, affiliated with the United Methodist Church, has produced graduates who lead the public and private sector. From boardrooms and research labs, to clinics and professional offices, the University's administration, led by President Robert Henry, has never lost the vision of its founders to maintain an institution in which students grow intellectually, spiritually, and morally.

The mission of Oklahoma City University School of Law is to prepare students to become responsible professionals through a rigorous program of instruction. Six core beliefs guide the instruction that focuses on students' intellectual and professional development, enabling them to become leaders in law, business, government and civic life. The core beliefs are:

academic excellence

personal and intensive attention

professionalism

service to the legal community

diversity of experience and viewpoint

student success and welfare

Hannah Diggs Atkins, '85, was the first African American woman elected to the Oklahoma House of Representatives. She also served as Oklahoma Secretary of State and Secretary of Social Services.

7 THE DOWNTOWN RENAISSANCE

No other American city has invested in its future like Oklahoma City has in the past three decades. In 1993, Mayor Ron Norick, the Oklahoma City Chamber of Commerce, and business and government leaders recognized that Oklahoma City was not competing well with other cities in attracting jobs and bettering its quality of life. Then, the idea of MAPS (Metropolitan Area Projects) was born.

Under Mayor Norick's leadership, Oklahoma City became the first city in the nation to undertake a public facilities improvement project the size of the MAPS program in 1993. Voters approved a one-cent sales tax to pay for a 20,000 seat indoor sports arena, a downtown ballpark, a new downtown library, construction of the Bricktown Canal, filling the North Canadian, now the Oklahoma River, with water, and renovations of the Civic Center Music Hall, Oklahoma State Fairgrounds, and the Cox Convention Center. The beauty of the investment plan was that projects would be paid for by cash, with no long-term debt incurred.

The Chesapeake Arena, home to the Oklahoma City Thunder, was made possible by the original MAPS vote. Bringing an NBA team to Oklahoma City excited fans beyond anyone's imagination and brought immense positive national publicity to the city. It is the hottest ticket in town. *Courtesy Oklahoma Publishing Company.*

The Bricktown Canal. *Courtesy Oklahoma Publishing Company.*

In 2001, voters approved MAPS for Kids, a $700 million package to upgrade Oklahoma City's public schools. In 2009, MAPS 3 was approved as a short-term penny sales tax to literally change the face of the downtown area, including a new convention center, a central park, and a light railway street car system. In September 2013, the Oklahoma City Council adopted a route for the street car running immediately adjacent to the new home of Oklahoma City University School of Law. Current plans call for a street car stop at the law school campus.

The relocation of the law school downtown perfectly fits the renaissance of the city. More than 30 percent of the 2012 entering students at the School of Law lived in the downtown area. The School of Law is a vital higher education component of the overall downtown redevelopment. Mayor Mick Cornett said:

> The will to invest in our community was born of a need to attract and retain talent to urban areas with a quality place. As Oklahoma City maps its future, creating an urban core that attracts this young, creative, mobile, highly-educated talent pool is top of mind.

In addition to specific improvements to downtown, several other areas of Oklahoma City near the new law school are literally exploding with development as part of the city's renaissance. Redevelopment plans created by city planners and private developers all recognize the importance of a higher education component. Dean Couch said, "That is why Oklahoma City University School of Law is such a good fit in the old Central High building. We are an integral part of the growth of the central section of the capital city."

The Oklahoma River has attracted large scale shore development and is host to a world-class U.S. Olympic rowing training center. *Courtesy Oklahoma Publishing Company.*

A renaissance is occurring in the Midtown area of Oklahoma City, just northwest of downtown. *Courtesy Midtown Renaissance.*

The Midtown area lay dormant for many years. Now it is home to apartment buildings, a variety of new restaurants, new streets, and new offices in the area that features St. Anthony Hospital. Capitalizing on the historic renaissance, private developers offer historic, architecturally unique properties to

The old Kaiser's Ice Cream Parlour is a focal point of the renaissance occurring in Midtown. *Courtesy Oklahoma Publishing Company.*

businesses and residents relocating to Midtown. Fully refurbished, remodeled properties are home to offices, restaurants, retail and residential living space. Located in the heart of Midtown's entertainment and restaurant district, properties offer chic urban living and upscale amenities.

MAPS projects literally put Bricktown on the map. Bricktown has become Oklahoma City's premiere entertainment district. For several decades the warehouse district sat dilapidated and underused. With the passage of the MAPS initiative in 1993, the City of Oklahoma City constructed a one-mile canal that connects the north Bricktown area with the Chesapeake Boathouse along the Oklahoma River. In the last decade, the Chickasaw Bricktown Ballpark is surrounded by restaurants and offices that have moved into Bricktown making the district one of the most unique areas in the state.

Automobile Alley, which runs along North Broadway from 4th Street to 13th Street, is a mixed-use neighborhood of offices, residences, loft apartments, restaurants, and retail. Beginning

in the 1920s, Broadway became known for the more than 50 automobile dealers located in the area. Over time, the area went into decline, but today, the district is enjoying an economic resurgence and revitalization along with the rest of downtown. The Oklahoma Contemporary Arts Center, a landmark building at Northwest 12th Street and Broadway Avenue, is expected to open in 2020.

The Arts District is home to several cultural destinations, including the Civic Center Music Hall, the Oklahoma City Museum of Art, the Ronald J. Norick Downtown Library, and the newly-renovated Myriad Botanical Gardens and Crystal Bridge Tropical Conservatory. The Civic Center Music Hall features a unique art deco motif and is a popular venue for concerts and other performing arts events. The Oklahoma City Museum of Art showcases notable paintings and pieces of sculpture, including the largest display of Dale Chihuly glass in the world. Project 180 street improvements currently underway will enhance the

Deep Deuce is alive and well. *Courtesy Oklahoma Publishing Company.*

Bricktown during the Christmas season. *Courtesy Oklahoma Publishing Company.*

The Oklahoma City University School of Law is an integral part of a fresh and new central section of Oklahoma City. *Courtesy Midtown Renaissance.*

district's appearance and create a better environment for walking and bicycling downtown.

Known for its African-American heritage, Deep Deuce is an urban neighborhood located north of Bricktown. During the 1940s and 1950s, the area was a hotbed of jazz music and African-American culture. Today, the neighborhood is undergoing a renaissance with many large-scale apartments and condominiums. The historic Calvary Baptist Church remains in the neighborhood as a community treasure and was recently renovated into a law firm.

8 A LAW SCHOOL IN PARTNERSHIP WITH THE COMMUNITY

Long-term planners of Oklahoma City could not have envisioned a more perfect location for the law school than the building that once housed Oklahoma City's first high school. The entire block bounded by Northwest Seventh Street on the south, Northwest Eighth Street on the north, Harvey Avenue on the west, and Robinson Avenue on the east is across the street from the Alfred P. Murrah Building, which replaced the former building destroyed in the 1995 bombing.

A blending of what the building looked like in 1927, on the left, and in 2014. Courtesy Oklahoma Historical Society, Greater Oklahoma City Chamber of Commerce, and Ackerman McQueen.

The former Central High building is one block north of the Oklahoma Department of Environmental Quality, two blocks north of the Oklahoma City National Memorial & Museum, and only a few blocks from the U.S. Courthouse, the Oklahoma County Courthouse, the county jail, and City Hall. Within a mile are literally thousands of venues for legal jobs, in private law firms, federal and state courts, and with local, state, and federal government agencies.

The law school capitalized on its central location and strengthened its role as the city's law school by launching the Norick Municipal Law Research Clinic in the spring of 2016. The clinic is a partnership with the City of Oklahoma City Municipal Counselor's Office. Students enrolled in the clinic develop research, writing, and communication skills by answering in-depth questions presented by the Municipal Counselor's Office. The clinic is the first of its kind in the nation and is named for former Oklahoma City mayor and past-chair of the Oklahoma City University Board of Trustees, the Honorable Ronald J. Norick.

The building's location is easily accessible from the major traffic arteries serving central Oklahoma. Interstate 235, which provides quick access to Interstates 35 and 40, is only four blocks east. A stop for the Oklahoma City Streetcar is located at the law

A regular stop on the Oklahoma City streetcar line is at OCU Law.

Members of the OCU Law building committee on the day of the building's grand opening.

school's campus at the corner of Robinson Avenue and Seventh Street. Students and faculty use the streetcar to quickly access courthouses, law firms, and other legal employers along the streetcar's route. No other law school is located so conveniently in the heart of the Heartland.

The law school building is a five-level structure containing approximately 177,296 square feet. Nearby are the Central Business District, Midtown, and Bricktown. The building itself occupies a full city block with 312 parking spaces. With parking lots and land on Northwest Seventh and Northwest Eighth streets, the total land area is slightly more than five acres.

It is an understatement to say the Central High School building is architecturally impressive. The original classical and gothic architecture building has been updated on the west side by creating a plaza on the second level above covered parking on the ground level.

The building contains many features desirable for a school of law. There are large common areas, wide hallways, numerous meeting rooms, and a theater-style presentation area. The finishes in the building are of the highest quality. Ceilings are ten-feet high and doors are nine-feet in most areas. Numerous glass walls allow natural light to flow into offices and corridors.

The building has four passenger elevators and one freight elevator for easy access. The former auditorium of Central High has been turned into McLaughlin Hall, a grand space that serves as a gathering place for students and faculty and a venue for major law school events. Although the building has been used for office space for three decades, renovations restored this beautiful historic structure to its original intended use as a place of learning.

The award-winning Oklahoma City architectural firm, FSB Architects & Engineers, developed a comprehensive plan for renovating the building. The firm has several interesting connections with the building's history. The firm designed a renovation to the building's west plaza in the 1980s. A member of the firm, Architect Lowe Runkle, who participated in the renovation design, is the great grandson of the building's original architect, Solomon Andrew Layton. When asked about the connection with his great grandfather Runkle said, "He was a pioneer, and he did many wonderful things. We've done a disservice to him tearing down his many wonderful buildings. We very much live in a disposable society, so to preserve a great piece of architectural history like this is exciting."

In October, 2013, the contract to renovate the building was awarded to the Oklahoma City construction firm of Anderson

& House. The construction firm, originally known as Campbell & Price, has a long-standing connection with the Central High building. Campbell & Price was the construction firm that built Central High in the early part of the previous century. And Anderson & House was hired by Southwestern Bell to repair the building after it was damaged in the 1995 bombing of the Alfred P. Murrah Federal Building. Anderson & House President Chris Wilson described the building after the bombing; "The windows were severely damaged; the ceiling was damaged, as were the floor tiles inside. But the building survived [the blast] very well. The exterior, built with cast stone, had minimal or no damage. It was built like a rock."

A Law School Designed for Learning

Planning for the building's transformation from corporate office space back into a school began in earnest after the purchase was completed. The library and other law school spaces were intentionally designed to encourage learning. This approach was pioneered by Yale University Librarian Emeritus Scott Bennett over the past decade but had yet to be applied in legal education. The design for learning technique was used to create spaces that help students become self-conscious and self-directed in their learning. This type of learning is called "intentional learning," and the landmark 2007 Carnegie Foundation for the Advancement of Teaching's report *Educating Lawyers* recommended its implementation in legal education.

Designing for learning began with student and faculty surveys to determine what intentional learning behaviors were most important. Studying alone outside of class ranked highest followed by several variations on collaboration. The survey also asked students and faculty to rank the types of spaces that best supported these learning behaviors. A café, learning commons, and study rooms emerged as highly supportive of collaboration. Carrels and study rooms were found to support silent study outside of class.

FIRST FLOOR
The Gaylord Family Learning Commons

The library spaces in the building began to take shape based on the survey results. The first floor was designed as a noisy, collaborative place featuring the Gaylord Family Learning Commons. A learning commons is space that brings students, faculty, academic and IT support, and librarians together around shared-learning tasks. Learning commons have been popular in university libraries for several years and are slowly being implemented in academic law libraries.

The Gaylord Family Learning Commons is the first learning commons to be constructed inside a law school library. Amenities are strategically placed in the learning commons to draw students, faculty, and others in and create "planned collisions." Planned collisions are chance encounters between members of a law school community purposefully created through design choices. Informal interactions lead to discussions about one another's work and create what space planners call "knowledge spillovers."

The Gaylord Family Learning Commons encompasses nearly 4,500 square feet of space on the library's first floor. The

The Gaylord Family Learning Commons as viewed from the second floor main entrance. *Courtesy Ann Sherman.*

commons features a full service café, open to the public. The learning commons integrates café space, the Homsey Family Technology Suite, and William C. Mee Computer Lab.

Café

The café is more than just a place for food and drink. It is a vibrant hub of activity located inside the bustling first floor learning commons. The design of the café encourages collaborative discussions and builds a sense of community among students, faculty and members of the nearby legal community.

The café includes various types of seating designed to encourage collaboration. Seating includes traditional café tables for small groups, a bar-height collaboration station, and data diner booths with flat screen monitors and connections for laptops. Casual discussions that start in the noisy café space lead to quieter study in the collaboration and study rooms adjacent to the café. The café features full service food and beverage service during normal operating hours. During the evenings vending machines provide sustenance for late night study sessions. Refrigerators and microwaves are also available for student use near the café.

Gerald and Jane Jayroe Gamble Library Classroom

A 600-square-foot open-plan library classroom is adjacent to the learning commons. This space includes furniture on casters that can be easily configured to support various instructional environments. Large glass doors visually connect the classroom with the learning commons while providing a quiet space during instructional sessions.

Law students studying at the café data diner booths. *Courtesy Ann Sherman.*

Professors Emeriti Daniel Morgan and Vicki MacDougall enjoy lunch. *Courtesy Ann Sherman.*

The classroom features a large flat-screen monitor, white boards, and power connectivity at each seat. The librarians use this space to deliver legal research instruction including the popular Award of Accomplishment in Legal Research Skills program. When the learning lab is not used for instruction, it is available for student use as a large group study room.

Kerr Foundation and Bob Burke Collaboration Suites

The learning commons features two collaboration suites. These open-plan study rooms feature moveable furniture on casters to encourage students and faculty to shape the space to suit their needs. Collaboration suites include the latest in educational

Computer lab. *Courtesy Kathryn Broad.*

Collaboration Suite. *Courtesy Kathryn Broad.*

technology including a large flat-screen monitor configured to simultaneously display content from multiple devices. Glass walls visually connect the suite with the learning commons while providing a quiet space for small group work. The suites include ample power and Wi-Fi connectivity.

William C. Mee Computer Lab

The William C. Mee Computer Lab is adjacent to the learning commons. The lab features a dramatic design with glass walls and a two-story high ceiling. The lab is highly visible from the learning commons and also from the school's main entrance on the second floor. The lab includes a large flat screen monitor and is used to provide legal research instruction. The lab is adjacent to the Homsey Family Technology Suite.

Other student amenities on the first floor include approximately 600 large lockers, showers for students who commute to the building on foot or by bicycle, and a lactation room. The lactation room was made possible through the generosity of Cathy and Adam Christensen.

Locker Hall was made possible through the generosity of the Midtown Renaissance Group and Bob Howard. *Courtesy Kathryn Broad.*

The Gary and Sue Homsey Plaza hosts an alumni gathering during the H&8th Night Market.

SECOND FLOOR

Gary and Sue Homsey Plaza and Homsey Family Lobby

The Gary and Sue Homsey Plaza and Homsey Family Lobby serve as the main entrance to the law school. The plaza contains outdoor furniture and offers commanding views of the downtown skyline and burgeoning Midtown district. The plaza hosts numerous outdoor functions including law school events connected with the H&8th Night Market, a street festival that draws 40,000 participants.

Students study on the Gary and Sue Homsey Plaza. Courtesy Ann Sherman.

SKYLINE TIMELINE

In 2015, OCU Law was selected as the site for a major temporary public art installation funded by Downtown OKC Inc.'s Artist Invitational Program. Artist Adam Lanman's "Skyline Timeline" proposal was chosen for the Gary and Sue Homsey Plaza. Lanman explained his work:, "Skyline Timeline is first and foremost a conceptual art work that displays a timeline of historic information concerning downtown Oklahoma City development. The project embraces the constant state of change from which our present environment emerges." The timeline covers five categories of events in a 60-year range beginning in 1956 and ending in 2015. Each tower of the artwork has ten panels. The panels are arranged by year beginning at the bottom of each tower and ending at the top in chronological order. The northern-most tower is the starting point for the timeline with the bottom panel of the north tower representing 1956. The color of each panel represents a category of information represented.

    Red: Building and Planning related events in and around OKC
    Blue: Policy and Legal issues affecting OKC development
    Yellow: Arts, Entertainment and Cultural events in OKC
    Green: Economic events and occurrences affecting OKC
    White: Unforeseen and unexpected events affecting OKC

Chickasaw Nation Law Library

The Chickasaw Nation Law Library is frequently filled with students engaged in group and quiet study. Students engage librarians at the circulation desk and at a reference collaboration station. Abundant natural light fills the reference reading room from skylight shafts. The reading room combines traditional wood study tables topped with reading lamps and leather club chairs, with the latest in technology including iPads for student use, a book self-checkout station, and a lay-flat book scanner. The reference collection is housed in custom millwork shelving designed specifically for the space.

Silent study areas are located around the perimeter of the second floor which receives abundant natural light from the building's recently replaced windows. Carrels ring the exterior walls and enjoy street-level views of the surrounding neighborhood. Lighting was upgraded to LED fixtures shortly after occupancy to increase the amount of light at reading tables.

The reference reading room of the Chickasaw Nation Law Library. *Courtesy Kathryn Broad.*

The reference room of the Chickasaw Nation Library is a favorite meeting place for students whether studying for finals or researching for papers or other projects. *Courtesy Ann Sherman.*

Steve and Carol Goetzinger Law Library Collection

The library's print and electronic collections are an important resource for law students and faculty, the local legal community, and the citizens of Oklahoma City. The collection is located primarily on the library's second floor in approximately 13,000 linear feet of compact shelving.

A silent study area adjacent to the Steve and Carol Goetzinger Law Library Collection. *Courtesy Ann Sherman.*

The library's reference, Oklahoma, and Native American collections are located in traditional open shelving around the second floor. The Native American Collection is the library's most prominent special collection. It contains print and electronic resources covering a wide range of legal issues relevant to

Students study in the library's reference collection

Native American law. The collection includes information about tribes associated with Oklahoma and beyond. The collection also includes significant works of art donated by Oklahoma City University President Robert Henry and University General Counsel Casey Ross.

The library shares the second floor with the Joe and Charlotte Edwards Law Review Suite, American Indian Law and Sovereignty Center, and Jodi G. Marquette American Indian Wills Clinic. Close physical proximity will only enhance the library's longstanding outreach efforts to these departments. The library's Native American print collection is strategically placed in open shelving adjacent to the Sovereignty Center and Wills Clinic. Locating this collection next to the academic programs it supports taps into the collection's place making power to encourage serendipity and connect patrons with their community and its values.

The Joe and Charlotte Edwards Law Review Suite includes spaces for individual work and collaboration. *Courtesy Kathryn Broad.*

A faculty member observes as students develop client interviewing skills in the Jodi G. Marquette American Indian Wills Clinic. *Courtesy Kathryn Broad.*

SPECIAL COLLECTIONS

Memorial Institute for the Prevention of Terrorism and Sloan Collections

In December, 2013, the law library acquired several collections previously housed at the Memorial Institute for the Prevention of Terrorism (MIPT). The collections include legal, political science, and international relations materials. The papers of noted terrorism expert Stephen Sloan and materials donated by the Lawson family to the MIPT are also included. These collections support the work of the school's Murrah Center for Homeland Security Law and Policy.

The library's Health Law Collection was created in 2011 with the input of Health Law Certificate Director Professor Emeritus Vicki MacDougall. The collection features print and electronic resources focusing on health law issues, genetics, bioethics, and related subjects.

The library is in the process of indexing and organizing the Judicial Papers of the Honorable Robert Henry. This collection is currently stored in approximately two hundred banker boxes.

The Bob Burke Supreme Court Autograph Collection has been digitized and is available from the law library's website. It is the nation's largest collection of autographs and writings of Justices of the U.S. Supreme Court.

The Justice Marian P. Opala Collection includes plaques, awards, and ephemera donated by Justice Opala to the school before his death in 2010.

The Oklahoma Collection includes statutes and legislative materials, administrative law materials, CLE materials, and treatises.

Center, OCU President Robert Henry, Dean Valerie Couch, and Oklahoma City Mayor Mick Cornett share the honors of cutting the ribbon at the Grand Opening of the new renovated law school. Cornett's father, Carroll E. Cornett, attended Central High School. *Courtesy Ann Sherman.*

THIRD FLOOR
McLaughlin Hall

The building's third floor was originally used as the main entrance to the high school. Stately entrances lead to the third floor from Robinson, Seventh, and Eighth streets. The former high school auditorium at the center of the third floor was transformed into the Paul and Jonalee McLaughlin Hall. The original ornately detailed proscenium arch was preserved as a key architectural feature of the space. McLaughlin Hall features a mix of tables and soft seating. It functions as the law school's living room, providing a space for students, faculty, and staff to casually interact with one another.

David Holt '09 received the law school's 2016 Young Alumni Award.

McLaughlin Hall is also used for large law school functions. *Courtesy Ann Sherman.*

Conservators install the restored murals. *Courtesy Simon Hurst.*

The Museum Room with the Olinka Hrdy murals. *Courtesy Simon Hurst.*

Museum

The museum is perhaps the most historically significant space in the entire building. Located on the third floor, the room's double glass doors open onto McLaughlin Hall. For special occasions, the room's second entrance is opened to Robinson Avenue, featuring a grand staircase, ornate iron, a gate, and marble-lined vestibule.

The room includes many high-quality finishes that are original to the building. The mosaic tile floor includes images symbolizing the building's original function as a high school. The walls feature marble wainscoting and built-in glass display cases housing memorabilia from the law school and Central High School. Classical sculptures on pedestals flank the display cases.

The crown jewels of the museum room are two large murals painted by Oklahoma artist Olinka Hrdy in 1928. Hrdy, Oklahoma's first modern artist, collaborated with Frank Lloyd

Wright at his Taliesin Studio. She painted art deco murals that once adorned a Tulsa building designed by Wright's protégé but have since mysteriously vanished. The murals in the law school's museum are extremely rare, as most of Hrdy's other murals were destroyed. Only one other Hrdy mural exists and is located in California. Associate Dean of Administration and Distance Education and Law Library Professor Jennifer Prilliman took the lead in ensuring the preservation of the Hrdy murals. The murals were restored and re-installed shortly before the building's opening. The Oklahoma Museum Association recognized Professor Prilliman's efforts by bestowing its 2015 Outstanding Conservation or Preservation Award to the School of Law for the conservation of the murals.

The restoration and ongoing preservation of the murals was made possible by the generous gift of Richard Sias in honor of Jeannette Sias. Additional support was provided by the Oklahoma City Foundation for Architecture.

Chesapeake Energy Careers Center

The careers center is immediately adjacent to McLaughlin Hall and is highly visible to students. The center's location in the southwest corner of the building provides impressive views of the downtown skyline. The center includes a reception area, resource room, and offices for the Associate Dean for Career Services and staff. The faculty member with responsibility for externships has an office inside the center. The Robert & Jan Henry Dignitary Suite is adjacent to the careers center to encourage interaction between students and visiting dignitaries. Nearby conference rooms are used for on-campus interviews and other programs and activities organized by the office.

Courtesy Kathryn Broad.

Academic Services Suite

This suite includes important points of services for students including the registrar and student services offices. Appropriately, the student services suite is located in a convenient and highly visible location opening onto McLaughlin Hall. The suite includes offices for the student services department personnel, copy and file rooms. Offices for members of the academic achievement department and financial aid/student accounts are also located inside the suite. Locating these offices inside the suite is convenient for students who are frequently referred to the academic achievement and financial aid departments by student services personnel.

Sarkeys Admissions Suite

The Sarkeys Admissions Suite is located in the northeast corner of the building immediately adjacent to the third floor grand hall. Prospective students can easily access the suite via the Eighth Street grand entrance after parking in the dedicated surface lots north of the building.

The suite includes offices for the Associate Dean for Admissions, law student ambassadors, admissions staff, and a work and file room. A corridor connecting the admissions suite with the student services suite is useful for introducing prospective students to the financial aid, academic support, and student services departments.

Courtesy Kathryn Broad.

The Couch family and Artist Benjamin Harjo pose with *Patterns of Change*. This painting will be permanently displayed in the gallery and was commissioned by the Class of 2017 and friends of Dean Emeritus Couch.

The Dean Valerie & Dr. Joseph Couch Art Gallery

The Gallery spans the width of the north side of the building's third floor. It was conceived as a space to host rotating exhibitions of artwork. The gallery has hosted an exhibit created by the Girl Scouts of Western Oklahoma featuring work of young women incarcerated in the Oklahoma County Juvenile Detention Center and an exhibit of architectural photography curated by the International Photography Hall of Fame.

Students gather in the G.T. and Elizabeth Blankenship Student Bar Association Center. *Courtesy Ann Sherman.*

G.T. and Elizabeth Blankenship Student Bar Association Center

The student bar association center is a hub of activity for the executive board of the student bar and various other law student organizations. These organizations provide opportunities for students to increase their knowledge in specific areas of law, gain leadership experience, and work closely with fellow students, faculty, alumni, and other legal professionals with similar passions. The center features a common area with work tables used for group meetings and projects. Lockers assigned to specific student organizations provide space for storing organizational materials. The center includes two offices shared by the bar association executive board members.

Crowe & Dunlevy Commons

The Crowe & Dunlevy Commons features two seminar rooms located on the building's third floor. A room divider can be retracted to combine both spaces into a single large seminar room or special events space. All seminar room furniture is on casters and can be easily configured to support various instructional environments. Each room is equipped with the latest in instructional technology controlled from a custom-designed smart podium. Power is provided at each seat for laptop computers. Large windows fill each seminar room with ample amounts of natural light. Mechanized solar shades are utilized for climate and glare control.

Dean Lee Peoples speaks to students and lawyers gathered in the Crowe & Dunlevy Commons for a Capital City Connect program in 2017.

The 2018 Homeland Security Law Summit.

Executive Director Emeritus of the Oklahoma Innocence Project, Vicki Behenna, right, visits with the project's two most recent exonerees, De'Marchoe Carpenter and Malcolm Scott.

Judge Alfred P. Murrah Center for Homeland Security Law and Policy

The Judge Alfred P. Murrah Center for Homeland Security Law and Policy is located on the third floor. The center was launched in early 2015 to examine the unique legal issues central to protecting and securing our nation, with a focus on the prevention of domestic terrorism. In partnership with the Oklahoma City National Memorial & Museum, the Murrah Center provides legal analysis, insight and support on matters of domestic security and counterterrorism and explores ways to combat extremism and radicalism at its root. The center houses the papers of noted terrorism expert Stephen Sloan.

Oklahoma Innocence Project

The Oklahoma Innocence Project is located in offices on the building's third floor. The project's space includes secure file storage, staff and student offices, and a conference room.

Professor Michael Gibson visits with students outside his office.

FOURTH FLOOR

Bill and Pam Shdeed Dean's Suite

The Dean of the School of Law and administrative staff are located on the fourth floor in a suite of offices that includes a reception area, work spaces and several conference rooms. This space is immediately adjacent to an open area with a view of McLaughlin Hall below where students and faculty gather on a daily basis.

Faculty Offices

Faculty offices are located on the perimeter of the building's fourth floor. Locating all faculty members on the same floor makes it easier for students to consult with faculty members. Faculty members have convenient access to their administrative assistants who are located in offices interspersed throughout the fourth floor. Open-plan gathering spaces filled with soft seating are immediately adjacent to the offices. These spaces host frequent meetings with students, alumni and faculty members. Two kitchenette/coffee bars are immediately adjacent to these areas.

John and Charlotte Richels Advancement and External Relations Suite

An office for the Assistant Dean for Advancement and External Relations is located in this suite. Offices for the Director of Alumni Relations, the Director of Special Events, and the Director of Communications and Marketing are located nearby.

J. William "Bill" Conger's law partner, Drew Neville, delivers remarks following the courtroom dedication and unveiling of Conger's portrait. *Courtesy Ann Sherman.*

FIFTH FLOOR
Inasmuch Foundation Learning Level
J. William Conger Courtroom

The J. William Conger Courtroom is the showplace of the Inasmuch Foundation Learning Level. The faculty chose to designate substantial contributions to the building campaign for the courtroom and to name the courtroom in honor of Professor Conger who died January 1, 2013. Dean Couch surprised Professor Conger at the 2012 Law Gala with the announcement of the naming of the courtroom. Conger was visibly moved by the honor and said, "I have been blessed with a wonderful life in the law, but this is the pinnacle of my career."

The courtroom is actively used in the school's advocacy curriculum and hosts occasional live trial and appellate court proceedings. Special features are incorporated into the design to accommodate actual court proceedings including a judges' chambers, jury deliberation room, and secure evidence storage room.

The courtroom includes majestic finishes and furnishings. The walls are lined with wood paneling, and custom millwork is used for the judge's bench, jury box, and counsel rail. The audience gallery includes seating for sixty. Floor to ceiling windows fill the space with ample natural light.

The latest in audio and video technology currently used in trial and appellate courtrooms is incorporated into this traditionally appointed space. The podium and counsel tables include connections for computers, document cameras, and other technology. Flat screen monitors allow the judge, jury, and audience members to view evidence and other presentation materials. Faculty or presiding judges have complete control over the system from the bench.

Video capture technology is integrated throughout the courtroom and jury deliberation room. This allows students and faculty in advocacy courses to review and evaluate video of mock trials and other proceedings. The video capture system also permits simulcasting of trial and appellate court proceedings to overflow crowds in the auditorium and other classrooms.

Auditorium

The auditorium space is believed to be original to the building. It seats approximately 75 in tiered theater-style seats and is used as a venue for hosting guest speakers. Legal scholars invited as the school's annual Brennan and Quinlan lecturers deliver their remarks in the theater room. The space is equipped with a large screen capable of displaying simulcast proceedings from the J. William Conger Courtroom to overflow crowds. The theater room also plays host to numerous guest speakers from the community invited to address the school's many student organizations.

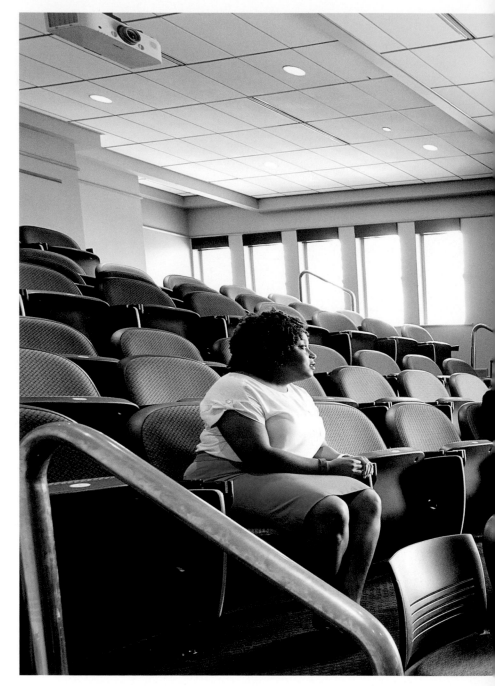

The auditorium is an important component of the school's educational spaces. *Courtesy Kathryn Broad.*

OCU Board of Trustees Chairman Ron Norick, left, at the unveiling of his portrait with artist Mike Wimmer. The portrait hangs in the Ron and Kandy Norick Lecture Hall.

Lecture Halls and Classrooms

Three large lecture halls and four medium-sized classrooms are located on the Inasmuch Learning Level. Seating is arranged in a tiered horseshoe configuration. This arrangement plays an important role in the educational experience by permitting students to see and converse with one another. The tiered horseshoe configuration allows faculty members to circulate easily among the students and encourages active engagement between students and faculty.

The lecture halls and classrooms are equipped with the latest in instructional technology controlled from a custom-designed smart podium. Built-in cameras and microphones are used for one-touch video recording at the option of each faculty member. Power is provided at each seat for laptops. Large windows fill each classroom with ample amounts of natural light. Mechanized solar shades are utilized for climate and glare control.

Vestibules and multiple entrances help control ambient hallway noise and assist with student circulation. The lecture halls are named for their generous benefactors, BancFirst, Ray and Pat Potts, and Ron and Kandy Norick. A classroom is named for Herman and LaDonna Meinders.

Seminar Rooms

Two seminar rooms located on the Inasmuch Learning Level can accommodate approximately 30 students each. All seminar room furniture is on casters and can be easily configured to support various instructional environments. Each room is equipped with the latest in instructional technology controlled from a custom-

The tiered, horseshoe arrangement in lecture halls allows students to easily engage each other and the professor during class. *Courtesy Ann Sherman.*

designed smart podium. Power is provided at each seat for laptops. Large windows will fill each seminar room with ample amounts of natural light. Mechanized solar shades are utilized for climate and glare control. Vestibules and multiple entrances help control ambient hallway noise and assist with student circulation. The seminar rooms are named for their generous benefactors, Randy and Connie Calvert and Norman & Edem Law Firm.

Conference Rooms and Study Rooms

Six conference rooms and twelve study rooms of varying size are located throughout the building. Touch screen displays outside of each room provide scheduling information. Most rooms are equipped with furniture that can be easily reconfigured into various arrangements. Large flat-screen wall-mounted monitors and white boards encourage collaboration. Each room provides ample power and Wi-Fi connectivity for laptop computers.

The following conference rooms are named for their generous benefactors:

Steven C. Agee Conference Room

Phil & Carolyn Hart Conference Room (Provided by Clark & Kay Musser)

The Kerr Foundation Conference Room

Phillips Murrah Conference Room

Bill & Pam Shdeed Dean's Conference Room

Hatton W. Sumners Conference Room

The following study rooms are named for their generous benefactors:

Andrew & Deborah Benton Study Room

Judge Dwain D. Box & Family Study Room

Mr. & Mrs. R.Y. Empire Study Room

Nicholas Harroz III Study Room

Steve & Carrie Katigan Study Room

Tom & Linda Klos Study Room

Eric T. Laity Study Room

Duke & Linda Ligon Study Room

KT & Marilyn Meade Study Room

Keri Coleman Norris Study Room

Tom Quinn Study Room

Steve & Marsha Turner Study Room

Offices were generously funded by the following benefactors:

Nancy & Bob Anthony

Dennis W. & JuChuan Arrow

Hamden & Robyn Baskin

Jim & Kay Bass

Joel Bieber

Joe & Kristin Carson

Bill Corum, Mike Brogan and Steve Garrett

Bill & Mary Ann Corum

Richard & Cynthia Dugger

Harry Goldman & Jettie Person

Gungoll Family

Linda Lambert

John MacKechnie

Robert Dean Gray & Deborah Watts McCormick

George Milner

Bob & Carol Naifeh

Michael O'Shea

Ralph Sallusti

Stuart & Pam Schroeder

Niles Jackson & Barbara Thornton

Casey Ross

Margaret Salyer

Tyler Family

Significant gifts received to support the School's programs since 2018 include:

Chickasaw Nation gift creating the Robert H. Henry Scholarship

Gaylord Family Foundation gift supporting the launch of the Center for Criminal Justice

Anonymous gift creating a scholarship in honor of Professor Alvin Harrell

The Munley Trial Advocacy program created by a gift of Chris and Bob Munley

The Oklahoma Bar Foundation and the Inasmuch Foundation gifts in support of the Housing Eviction Legal Assistance Program

The study rooms are an integral part of the learning level. *Courtesy Ann Sherman.*

EPILOGUE
A MIGHTY SPIRIT LIVES HERE

For decades, Oklahoma City University School of Law has been proud to serve as Oklahoma City's law school. Our move to the center of the City makes this dynamic, mutually beneficial connection abundantly clear. We have planted our law school in the heart of our thriving, growing city whose history, struggles, progress and great future we share. With this move, we dedicate ourselves anew to maintaining an enduring partnership with the City we love.

Oklahoma City University School of Law: Come to Learn. Learn to Lead. brings to life the history of our downtown building. Beginning in 1910 and for nearly six decades, the building at 800 North Harvey Avenue served as the City's landmark high school. Future leaders in business, law, government, education, and the arts received their high school education here. And generations of citizens have maintained their affection for this magnificent structure where their lives began to unfold. Now, over a century after its creation, this historic building returns to its original purpose as a place of learning.

The artful transformation of the building into a cutting edge law school has garnered recognition through three significant awards. Oklahoma City Mayor Mick Cornett honored the University's efforts and commitment through the 2015 City of Oklahoma City Mayor's Award for Outstanding Development and Preservation. Preservation Oklahoma bestowed on the project the Award for Excellence in Historical Preservation. And the Oklahoma Museums Association honored our conservation of the colorful 1928 Olinka Hrdy murals, now restored for the enjoyment of many generations to come. We are grateful for these awards and public recognition. They add to the immense satisfaction we are all experiencing as we enjoy daily the beauty, strength and inspiration of the building. Its architecture blends to perfection the serious civic purpose of education and the warm personality of a beloved space. We are finding it a perfect place to study, learn, think, read, analyze, debate, form opinions, change opinions, solve problems, provide leadership, develop professional strengths, create enduring friendships and, most comprehensively, build a community.

I thank Bob Burke and Professor Lee Peoples for their stewardship to this building. In this book, they have beautifully captured its history and its people. They show us that a mighty spirit lives here. And in this place, we proudly move forward in the spirit of progress -- where tradition, innovation, leadership and service define both our heritage and our future.

Valerie Couch
Dean Emeritus and Professor of Law, Oklahoma City University
School of Law

Jim Roth '09, center, visiting with students at the Capital City Connect Energy Law Program. Roth served as co-chair for this event.

Judge Robert Bacharach of the United States Court of Appeals for the Tenth Circuit was the law school's 2017 McAfee Taft Distinguished Jurist in Residence.

A.V. Peoples, III, '74; J.R. Homsey, '73, and Interim Dean Lee Peoples at the law school Christmas Party in 2017.

McLaughlin Hall hosts an energy law conference with participants from several states.

Gary Homsey '74, Oklahoma Supreme Court Chief Justice Douglas Combs '76, Oklahoma County District Judge Don Andrews '89, James Gibbs, and Emmanuel Edem '82 speak at the CLE program, Civility Matters, hosted by the law school in 2017.

The inaugural group of OCU Law student volunteers training at Palomar headquarters.

THE PEOPLE OF OCU LAW

James A. "Jim" Roth '94 was named Dean of the Oklahoma City University School of Law in 2018. Roth previously practiced law with Phillips Murrah and served as county commissioner in Oklahoma County and as a member of the Oklahoma Corporation Commission.

DEANS

1907-1910:	C.B. Ames
1952-1957:	Roger Stephens
1957-1968:	John G. Hervey
1968-1973:	Ted Foster
1974-1976:	Richard E. Coulson
1977-1981:	Edward Palmer
1982-1983:	William Brian Martin
1984-1991:	Stuart S. Strasner
1991-1994:	Robert H. Henry
1995-1997:	Rennard Strickland
1998-2011:	Lawrence K. Hellman
2012-2017:	Valerie K. Couch
2018- :	James A. Roth

Robert Henry was dean of the law school from 1991 to 1994.

INTERIM DEANS

1973-1974:	Von Russel Creel
1976-1977:	Sylas Lyman
1981-1982:	Nancy I. Kenderdine
1983-1984:	Marjorie Downing
1994-1995:	Arthur G. LeFrancois
1997-1998:	Jay Conison
2011-2012:	Eric T. Laity
2017-2018:	Lee F. Peoples

Lawrence "Larry" Hellman served as law school dean from 1998 to 2011.

ASSOCIATE DEANS

1967-1969:	Ted Foster
1971-1973:	Richard E. Coulson
1973-1974:	Marjorie Downing
1974-1975:	Von Russel Creel
1975-1977:	Penn Lerblance
1977-1978:	Marjorie Downing
1978-1980:	Lawrence K. Hellman
1980-1981:	Nancy I. Kenderdine
1981-1982:	Vicki Lawrence MacDougall
1983-1984:	Dennis Arrow
1984-1987:	Daniel J. Morgan
1987-1991:	Frederick D. Lewis Jr.
1991-1993:	Arthur G. LeFrancois
1993-1997:	Jay Conison
1997-1999:	Nancy I. Kenderdine
1999-2003:	Norwood P. Beveridge
2003-2006:	Patricia Hatamyar
2006-2011:	Eric T. Laity
2011-2012:	Laurie Jones
2012-2017:	Eric T. Laity
2017- :	Paula J. Dalley

ASSOCIATE/ASSISTANT DEAN FOR STUDENTS

1992-1995:	Sonya S. Beckham
1995-1997:	Victor Cook
1997-1998:	Charles Cantrell
2000-2013:	Deborah Felice
2019- :	Alana Haynes House

ASSOCIATE DEAN OF LIBRARY AND TECHNOLOGY

2019- :	Lee F. Peoples

ASSOCIATE DEAN for ADMINISTRATION AND DISTANCE EDUCATION

2019- :	Jennifer Prilliman

ASSOCIATE DEAN/ASSISTANT DEAN/ DIRECTOR FOR ADMISSIONS

1981-1983:	Michael Decker
1983-1984:	Frederick Ross Ferguson
1984-1986:	Doug Hayes
1988-1998:	Gary D. Mercer
1998-2044:	Peter S. Storandt
2004-2007:	Tamara Martinez-Anderson
2007-2008:	Michael Johnson
2008-2012:	Bernard Jones
2012- :	Laurie Jones

ASSISTANT DEAN FOR PROFESSIONAL AND CAREER DEVELOPMENT

1993-1996:	Barbara Merritt
1996-2011:	Gina Rowsam
2011-2012:	Joshua Snavely (Interim)
2012-2018:	Pete Serrata
2018-2019:	Alana Haynes House
2019- :	Bianca J. Bryant (Director)

ASSISTANT DEAN FOR ADVANCEMENT

2002-2005:	Michael Sohn
2005-2010:	Marc Thompson
2010-2012:	Bernard Jones, Associate Dean
2012-2016:	Joshua Snavely
2016- :	Stephen Butler

REGISTRAR

1974-1982: Doris Jackson
1982-1985: Jane Smith
1985-1987: Doris Jackson
1987-1991: Gayle Robertson
1991-2004: Sharon Hayes
2004-2007: Melanie Brooks
2007-   : Shanna Pope

LIBRARY DIRECTORS

1961-1973: Lelin Eugene Pack
1973-1977: Patricia J. Higgons
1977-1979: Kent D. Talbot
1979-1984: William J. Beintema
1984-2010: Judith Morgan
2010-2017: Lee F. Peoples
2017-2018: Jennifer Prilliman, Interim
2018-:   Lee F. Peoples

EMERITUS FACULTY

John G. Hervey, deceased
A.D. Erdberg, deceased
Ted Foster, deceased
Fred J. McDonald, deceased
Silas R. Lyman, deceased
Marjorie Downing
Nancy I. Kenderdine
Judith Morgan
Norwood P. Beveridge
Richard Coulson, deceased
Von R. Creel
Daniel J. Morgan
Charles Cantrell

Arthur G. LeFrancois
Alvin C. Harrell
Dennis Arrow
Deborah Tussey
Peter Dillon
Phyllis Bernard
Lawrence K. Hellman
Vicki Lawrence MacDougall

DEAN EMERITUS

Lawrence K. Hellman
Valerie K. Couch

Even the young proudly wear an OCULaw tee shirt. Madeline Grace Hubbard is the daughter of law school alumnus Emily Biscone Hubbard and granddaughter of law school graduate Joe Biscone.

MAY COMMENCEMENT SPEAKERS

1998:   Robert A. Butkin, Oklahoma State Treasurer

1999:   William G. Paul, President Elect, American Bar Association

2000:   The Honorable Sven Erik Holmes, Judge, U.S. District Court, Northern District of Oklahoma

2001:   The Honorable Reta M. Strubhar, Judge, Oklahoma Court of Criminal Appeals

2002:   The Honorable N. Sanders Sauls, Circuit Judge for the Second Judicial Circuit of Florida

2003:   The Honorable Lee R. West, U.S. District Judge for the Western District of Oklahoma

2004:   The Honorable Ralph G. Thompson, Senior U.S. District Judge for the Western District of Oklahoma

2005:   The Honorable Tom Colbert, Justice of the Oklahoma Supreme Court

2006:   Emmanuel E. Edem '82 founding partner, Norman & Edem, Oklahoma City, OK

2007:   The Honorable Jerome A. Holmes, Judge of the Tenth U.S. Circuit Court of Appeals

2008:   The Honorable Stephanie Kulp Seymour, Senior Judge of the Tenth Circuit Court of Appeals

2009:   The Honorable Judge Vicki Miles-LaGrange, Chief Judge – U.S. District Court for the Western District of Oklahoma

2010:   The Honorable Brad Henry-Governor of Oklahoma

2011:   The Honorable Steven W. Taylor, Chief Justice, Supreme Court of Oklahoma

2012:   John W. Norman, Norman & Edem, P.L.L.C.

2013:   The Honorable Tom Colbert, Justice of the Oklahoma Supreme Court

2014:   Barry R. Grissom, U.S. Attorney, District of Kansas

2015:   John Richels, Chief Executive Officer, Devon Energy

2016:   The Honorable Vicki Miles-LaGrange, U.S. District Court, Western District of OK

2017:   Mike Turpen, Riggs, Abney, Neal, Turpen, Orbison and Lewis

2018:   Mickey Edwards, former Republican congressman, 5th District of Oklahoma

2019:   Brian Huseman, Vice President of Publich Policy, Amazon

DECEMBER COMMENCEMENT SPEAKERS

1998: Douglas W. Sanders, Jr., President-Elect, Oklahoma Bar Association

1999: M. Joe Crosthwait, Jr., President-Elect, Oklahoma Bar Association

2000: Charles D. "Buddy" Neal, Jr., President-Elect, Oklahoma Bar Association

2001: Gary C. Clark, President-Elect, Oklahoma Bar Association

2002: Melissa DeLacerda, President-Elect, Oklahoma Bar Association

2003: Harry A. Woods, Jr., President-Elect, Oklahoma Bar Association

2004: Michael D. Evans, President-Elect, Oklahoma Bar Association

2005: William R. Grimm, President-Elect, Oklahoma Bar Association

2006: James Winchester, Vice Chief Justice, Oklahoma Supreme Court

2007: J. William Conger, University Counsel and Distinguished Lecturer in Law, Oklahoma City University and President-Elect, Oklahoma Bar Association

2008: Jon K. Parsley, President-Elect, Oklahoma Bar Association

2009: Allen M. Smallwood, President-Elect, Oklahoma Bar Association

2010: Deborah Ann Reheard, President-Elect, Oklahoma Bar Association

2011: Cathy M. Christensen, President-Elect, Oklahoma Bar Association

2012: James T. Stuart, President-Elect, Oklahoma Bar Association

2013: Renee DeMoss, President-Elect, Oklahoma Bar Association

2014: No December Commencement

2015: Andrew K. Benton, President of Pepperdine University

DISTINGUISHED LAW ALUMNUS/A AWARD

1998–1999:	Douglas Sanders, Jr.
1999–2000:	Charles D. "Buddy" Neal, Jr.
2000–2001:	Ronald Howland
2001–2002:	M. Joe Crosthwait, Jr.
2003–2004:	Michael D. Brown
2004–2005:	Earl D. Mills
2005–2006:	Patricia D. MacGuigan
2006–2007:	Bob Burke
2007–2008:	Tom Quinn
2008–2009:	Richard Coulson
2009–2010:	No event, no award
2010–2011:	Robert Ravitz
2011–2012:	Christina Murray
2012–2013:	Barry Grissom
2013–2014:	Vicki Z. Behenna '84
2014–2015:	Gilbert K. Squires
2015–2016:	Andrew K. Benton '79
2016–2017:	Janie S. Hipp '84
2017–2018	No award given
2018–2019	Snadra Mitchell '88, Deputy Commissioner General United Nations

OUTSTANDING YOUNG ALUMNUS/A AWARD

2000–2001:	Linda Samuel-Jaha
2001–2002:	D. Renee Hildebrant
2003–2004:	Leslie L. Lynch
2004–2005:	Raymund C. King
2005–2006:	Keri C. Prince
2006–2007:	Abdul Zindani
2007–2008:	Christina E. Murray
2008–2009:	Donna Suchy
2009–2010:	Angela Morrison Uhland
2010–2011:	Brandon Long
2011–2012:	Beau Patterson
2012–2013:	Tynan Grayson
2013–2014:	The Honorable TW Shannon '04
2014–2015:	Lieutenant Governor Todd Lamb
2015–2016:	S. Rachel Pappy '08
2016–2017:	Senator David F. Holt '09
2017–2018:	No award given
2018–2019:	Monica Ybarra '14

MARIAN OPALA LIFETIME ACHIEVEMENT IN LAW AWARD

1999-2000:	Justice Marian Opala
2000-2001:	Richard F. McDivitt
2001-2002:	Judge Fred Daughtery
2003-2004:	Judge William J. Holloway, Jr.
2004-2005:	William G. Paul
2005-2006:	Judge Reta M. Strubhar
2006-2007:	Alvin Harrell
2007-2008:	John Green
2008-2009:	William Burkett
2009-2010:	No event, no award
2010-2011:	Judge Carol Hansen
2011-2012:	Judge Niles Jackson
2012-2013:	J. William Conger
2013-2014:	William F. Shdeed '65
2014-2015:	Judge Vicki Miles-LaGrange
2015-2016:	Ray H. Potts '65
2016-2017:	The Honorable Steven W. Taylor
2017-2018:	No award given
2018-2019:	Justice James Winchester '77

LAW FIRM OF DISTINCTION AWARD

1999-2000:	McKinney & Stringer
2000-2001:	Dunlap, Codding & Rogers
2001-2002:	McAfee & Taft
2003-2004:	Crowe & Dunlevy
2004-2005:	Norman & Edem
2005-2006:	Scoggins & Cross
2006-2007:	Phillips, McFall, McCaffrey, McVay & Murrah
2007-2008:	Hartzog Conger Cason & Neville
2008-2009:	Hall, Estill, Hardwick, Gable, Golden & Nelson
2009-2010:	No event, no award
2010-2011:	Gable Gotwals
2011-2012:	Hall Estill
2012-2013:	Derryberry & Naifeh
2013-2014:	Pierce Couch Hendrickson Baysinger & Green, LLP
2014-2015:	Williams Box Forshee & Bullard, P.C.
2015-2016:	Calvert Law Firm
2016-2017:	Fellers Snider
2017-2018:	No award given
2018-2019:	Riggs Abney

DISTINGUISHED SERVICE TO THE COMMUNITY AWARD

2003-2004:	William F. Shdeed, Jr.
2004-2005:	Yvonne Kauger
2005-2006:	M. Susie Magaw-Viele
2006-2007:	Nona M. Lee
2007-2008:	Ross A. Plourde
2008-2009:	Cathy Christensen
2009-2010:	No event, no award
2015-2016:	Oklahoma City National Memorial & Museum
2016-2017:	The Honorable Ronald J. Norick
2017-2018:	No award given
2018-2019	Elaine Turner '89

LAW REVIEW BANQUET SPEAKERS

2000:	The Honorable James Winchester
2001:	The Honorable Daniel J. Boudreau
2002:	William R. Burkett
2003:	The Honorable Nancy Coats
2004:	The Honorable James Edmondson
2005:	Martin Belsky
2006:	The Honorable Arlene Johnson
2007:	Attorney General, Drew Edmonson
2008:	Commissioner James A. Roth
2009:	The Honorable Deborah Browers Barnes
2010:	The Honorable Jerry Goodman
2011:	The Honorable Douglas L. Combs
2012:	Amy D. White
2013:	Hamden Baskin III
2014:	David L. Walling
2015:	Thomas M. Jones
2016:	Randall K. Calvert
2017:	Steve Korotash
2018:	The Honorable Scott Rowland
2019:	The Honorable Deborah Bowers Barnes and Gregg W. Lather

OUTSTANDING LAW REVIEW ALUMNUS/A AWARD RECIPIENTS

1997:	The Honorable Daniel L. Owens
1998:	Cynthia L. Sparling
1999:	Dennis R. Box
2000:	Vicki Lawrence MacDougall
2001:	Stuart R. Schroeder
2002:	Richard P. Propester
2003:	Mack K. Martin
2004:	Charles F. Moser
2005:	Norman A. Lofgren
2006:	The Honorable Carol P. Hubbard
2007:	Robert N. Sheets
2008:	Leonard Pataki
2009:	The Honorable Deborah Browers Barnes
2010:	Angela Morrison Uhland
2011:	W. Kelly Stewart
2012:	Amy D. White
2013:	Hamden Baskin III
2014:	David L. Walling
2015:	Thomas M. Jones
2016:	Randall K. Calvert
2017:	Steve Korotash
2018:	The Honorable Scott Rowland
2019:	The Honorable Deborah Browers Barnes
2019:	Gregg W. Luther

LAW DAY SPEAKERS 1999-2007

1992:	The Honorable Stanley Mosk
1993:	The Honorable Robin J. Cauthron
1994:	The Honorable Danny J. Boggs
1995:	The Honorable Vicki Miles-LaGrange
1996:	The Honorable Paul J. Kelly, Jr.
1999:	The Honorable Michael Daly Hawkins
2000:	The Honorable Susan Webber Wright
2001:	The Honorable Robert Benham
2002:	The Honorable Stephen Friot
2003:	Louis Henkin
2004:	Robert J. Grey, Jr.
2005:	Vanita Gupta
2006:	Steven Lubet
2007:	Counter Terrorism Symposium in Celebration of Law Day, The Honorable John Richter

MERIT SCHOLAR FACULTY MEMBER OF THE YEAR

2009:   Von Creel
2010:   Vicki MacDougall
2011:   Danne Johnson
2012:   Brendan Maher
2013:   Brendan Maher
2014:   Paula Dalley
2015:   Michael Gibson
2016:   Paula Dalley
2017:   Marc Blitz
2018:   Marc Blitz
2019:   No award given

QUINLAN LECTURERS

1981
Norval Morris
Julius Kreeger Professor of Law,
The University of Chicago

1982
Arthur R. Miller
Bruce Bromley Professor of Law
Harvard University

1983
James E. Bond
Professor of Law
Wake Forest University

1984
E. Allan Farnsworth
Alfred McCormack Professor of Law
Columbia University

1985
Franklin E. Zimring
Director, Earl Warren Legal Institute
University of California, Berkeley

1986
Morton J. Horwitz
Charles Warren Professor of American Legal History
Harvard University

1987
Sanford Levinson
Charles Tilford McCormack Professor of Law
University of Texas

1988
Richard A. Epstein
James Parker Hall Distinguished Service Professor
University of Chicago

1989
A.E. Dick Howard
White Burkett Professor of Law and Public Affairs
University of Virginia

1990
Leo Katz
Assistant Professor of Law
University of Michigan

1991
Bernard Grossfield
Professor of Law
University of Muenster

1992
The Honorable Antonin Scalia
Associate Justice, United States Supreme Court

1993
George Anastaplo
Professor of Law
Loyola University Chicago

1994
Bernard Schwartz
Chapman Distinguished Professor
University of Tulsa

1995
Deborah L. Rhode
Professor of Law and Director of the Center on Legal Ethics
Stanford University Law School

1996
Robert A. Williams, Jr.
Professor of Law and American Indian Studies
University of Arizona College of Law

1997
Taunya Lovell Banks
Jacob A. France Professor of Equality Jurisprudence
University of Maryland School of Law

1998
The Honorable John T. Noonan Jr.
Judge, United States Court of Appeals for the Ninth Circuit

1999
Bernard Bailyn
Adams University Professor Emeritus
Harvard University

2000
Charles Fried
Beneficial Professor of Law
Harvard University

2001
William B. Ewald
Professor of Law and Philosophy
University of Pennsylvania

2002
Dennis Patterson
Distinguished Professor of Law
Rutgers University School of Law (Camden)

2003
G. Edward White
University Professor, John B. Minor Professor of
Law and History, and Sullivan & Cromwell
Research Professor University of Virginia

2004
Phillip Bobbitt
A.W. Walker Centennial Chair in Law
University of Texas

2005
Charles J. Ogletree, Jr.
Jesse Climenko Professor of Law
Director of the Charles Hamilton Houston Institute
for Race and Justice Harvard Law School

2006
Noah Feldman
New York University Professor of Law
New American Foundation Fellow
Senior Adviser for Constitutional Law
Coalition Provisional Authority, Iraq, 2003

2007
Anita L. Allen
Henry R. Silverman Professor of Law and
Professor of Philosophy University of Pennsylvania
Law School

2008
Heather Gerken
Professor of Law
Yale Law School

2009
Reva Siegel
Professor of Law
Yale Law School

2011
Kathleen Sullivan
Professor of Law
Former Law School Dean Stanford University

2012
Pamela Karlan
Kenneth & Harle Montgomery Professor of Public
Interest
Law and Co-Director, Supreme Court Litigation Clinic
Stanford University

2013
Sarah Gordon
Arlin M. Adams Professor of Constitutional Law and
Professor of History
University of Pennsylvania Law School

2014
Judith Resnik
Arthur Liman Professor of Law
Yale Law School

2015
No Quinlan lecture – moved into new building

2016
Kenneth W. Mack
Inaugural Lawrence D. Biele Professor of Law
Harvard Law School

2017
Mary Bilder
Founders Professor of Law
Boston College Law School

2018
Joanne Freeman
Professor of History and American Studies
Yale University

2019
Danielle Keats Citro
Morton and Sophia Macht Professor of Law
Universit of Maryland Francis King Carey School of
Law

2020
Ashutosh A. Bhagwat
Boochever and Bird Endowed Chair for the Study
and Teaching of Freedom and Equality
Martin Luther King, Jr. Professor of Law
University of California, Davis, School of Law

BRENNAN LECTURERS

1997-1998 (Inaugural)
Hans A. Linde
Senior Judge
Oregon Supreme Court

1998-1999
Erwin Chemerinsky
Sydney M. Irmas Professor of Public Interest Law,
Legal Ethics, and Political Science
The University of Southern California College of Law

1999-2000
Michael W. McConnell
Presidential Professor of Law
University of Utah College Law

2000-2001
Robert F. Williams
Distinguished Professor of Law
Rutgers University School of Law

2001-2002
Elizabeth Garrett
Professor of Law
The University of Chicago

2002-2003
Christian G. Fritz
Professor of Law
University of New Mexico School of Law

2003-2004
William N. Eskridge, Jr.
John A. Garver Professor of Jurisprudence
Yale Law School

2004-2005
Randy Barnett
Austin B. Fletcher Professor
Boston University School of Law

2005-2006
Paul Finkelman
Chapman Distinguished Professor
University of Tulsa College of Law

2006-2007
Roderick M. Hills, Jr.
William T. Comfort, III Professor of Law
New York University School of Law

2007-2008
The Honorable Robert P. Young, Jr.
Justice of the Michigan Supreme Court

2008-2009
The Honorable Judge Jeffrey Sutton
United States Court of Appeals for the Sixth Circuit

2009-2010
Nicole Garnett
Professor of Law
University of Notre Dame Law School

2010-2011
Daniel Rodriguez
Minerva House Drysdale Regents Chair in Law
University of Texas School of Law

2011-2012
Clint Bolick
Director of Scharf-Norton Center for Constitutional
Litigation
Goldwater Institute

2012-2013
The Honorable Diane S. Sykes
United States Court of Appeals 7th Circuit

2013-2014
Ilya Somin
Professor of Law
George Mason University School of Law

2014-2015
No Brennan Lecture—moved into new building

2015-2016
John Dinan
Professor of Politics and International Affairs
Wake Forrest University

2016-2017
Brian Fitzpatrick
Professor of Law
Vanderbilt Law School

2017-2018
Josh Chafetz
Professor of Law
Cornell Law School

2018-2019
Sharmila Sohoni
Herzog Endowed Scholar and Professor of Law
University of San Diego School of Law

INTEGRIS HEALTH LAW & MEDICINE LECTURE SERIES

2010
Eleanor D. Kinney, Hall Render Professor of Law Emeritus & Co-director of the William S. and Christine S. Hall Center for Law and Health, Emeritus, Indiana University
The Real Truth about Death Panels: Comparative Effectiveness Research and the Health Reform Legislation

2011
Professor Keith Findley, Clinical Professor of Law, Wisconsin University Law School and Co-director of the Wisconsin Innocence Project
Challenging Shaken Baby Syndrome Convictions in Light of New Medical and Scientific Research

2013
Professor Maxwell Mehlman, Arthur E. Petersilge Professor of Law and Director of the Law-Medicine Center, Case School of Law, and Professor of Biomedical Ethics, Case School of Medicine
Extinction by Design: Genetic Engineering and the Future of Human Evolution

2017
Professor Nadia N. Sawicki, Professor of Law & Academic Director of the Beazley Institute for Health Law and Policy at Loyola University of Chicago
Protecting Physican Speech: Can We Rely on the First Ammendment?

2018
Professor Lori Andrews, Distinguished Professor of Law and Director of the Institute for Science, Law and Technology, Illinois Institute of Technology, Chicago-Kent College of Law
Genetics, Art & Policy

2019
Professor Michelle Bratcher Goodwin, Cancellor's Professor of Law, Director, Center for Biotechnology and Global Health Policy at University of California, Irvine School of Law
Fruits of the Flesh: The Complexities of the Informed Consent in a Modern Era

MCAFEE & TAFT JURIST-IN-RESIDENCE

2008
The Honorable Michael D. Hawkins, US Court of Appeals for the Ninth Circuit

2009
The Honorable Ruth V. McGregor, Chief Justice, Arizona Supreme Court

2010
The Honorable Neil Gorsuch, US Court of Appeals for the Tenth Circuit

2012 SPRING
The Honorable David Ebel, US Court of Appeals for the Tenth Circuit

2012 FALL
The Honorable The Honorable Michael R. Murphy, US Court of Appeals for the Tenth Circuit

2014
The Honorable Timothy Tymkovich, US Court of Appeals for the Tenth Circuit

2017
The Honorable Robert E. Bacharach, US Court of Appeals for the Tenth Circuit

DISTINGUISHED PRACTITIONER IN RESIDENCE

2017-2018
Jim Roth, Phillips Murrah, P.C.

2018-2019
Phil Busey, Delaware Resource Group

2019-2020
Nikki Edwards, Phillips Murrah, P.C.

The relocation of the OCU law school to downtown is far more significant than people may realize. The influx of hundreds of students and faculty will bring quite a bit of life to the neighborhood.

Steve Lackmeyer in *The Oklahoman*

BIBLIOGRAPHY AND SUGGESTED READING

NEWSPAPERS AND PERIODICALS

Harlow's Weekly, Oklahoma City, Oklahoma
Oklahoma City Downtown, Oklahoma City, Oklahoma
Oklahoma City Times, Oklahoma City, Oklahoma
Oklahoma Today, Oklahoma City, Oklahoma
The Daily Oklahoman, Oklahoma City, Oklahoma
The Oklahoma Journal, Oklahoma City, Oklahoma
The Sunday Oklahoman, Oklahoma City, Oklahoma

COLLECTIONS

Oklahoma Historical Society vertical files
Oklahoma Department of Libraries vertical files
Oklahoma Publishing Company Photograph Collection,
   Oklahoma Historical Society

BOOKS

Arnold, Anita. *Oklahoma City Music: Deep Deuce and
   Beyond*. Chicago: ArcadiaPublishing, 2010
Blackburn, Bob. L. *Heart of the Promised Land*: Oklahoma
   County. Woodland Hills, California: Windsor Publica-
   tions, Inc., 1982.
Burke, Bob. *Miracle at Guthrie: The Making of Oklahoma*.
Oklahoma City: Oklahoma Heritage Association, 2011.
Burke, Bob. *Oklahoma: The Center of It All*. Encino, Califor-
   nia: Cherbo Publishing, 2002.
Creel, Von Russell and Bob Burke. *Oklahoma City Univer-
   sity School of Law: A History*. Oklahoma City: Common-
   wealth Press, 2008.
Ellison, Ralph. *Going to the Territory*. New York: Random
   House, 1986.
Holt, David. *Big League City*. Oklahoma City: Full Circle
   Press, 2012.
Lackmeyer, Steve and Jack Money. *Operation Scissortail*.
   Oklahoma City: Full Circle Press, 2012.
Lambert, Paul F., Kenny A. Franks, and Bob Burke. *Historic
   Oklahoma*. Oklahoma City: Oklahoma Heritage Associ-
   ation, 1999.
Oklahoma Historical Society. *The Encyclopedia of Oklaho-
   ma History and Culture*.
Oklahoma City: 2008.
Stewart, Roy P. with Pendleton Woods, *Born Grown*. Okla-
   homa City: Fidelity Bank, 1974.
Wynn, Bradley. *Oklahoma City's Midtown*. Chicago: Arca-
   dia Publishing, 2014.

ACKNOWLEDGMENTS

The authors acknowledge the assistance of the
following individuals and institutions in this project:

Brook Arbeitman
Kathryn Broad
Assistant Dean for Advancement and
    External Relations Stephen Butler
Gini Moore Campbell
Von Russell Creel
Eric Dabney
Marcia Davis
Jim Thorpe Association
Honorable Yvonne Kauger
Natalie Nichole Taylor
Oklahoma Hall of Fame
Oklahoma Historical Society
Linda Lynn
Skip McKinstry
Cheryl Morgan
Lauren Stradinger
Cindy Elbah
Oklahoma Publishing Company
Oklahoma Sports Hall of Fame
Law Library Professor Jennifer Prilliman
Ann Sherman
Topps Inc.
Kris Vculek
William Welge
Lorraine Wright

INDEX